OUR HIDDEN HERITAGE

OUR HIDDEN HERITAGE

Five centuries of women artists

ELEANOR TUFTS

PADDINGTON PRESS LTD

THE TWO CONTINENTS PUBLISHING GROUP

To Hazel and James Tufts

ISBN 0-8467-0026-3
Library of Congress Catalog Card Number 73-20955
© Copyright 1974 Paddington Press Ltd
Printed in the U.S.A.
Second printing 1975

Designed by Richard Browner

IN THE UNITED STATES
PADDINGTON PRESS LTD
TWO CONTINENTS PUBLISHING GROUP
30 East 42 Street
New York City, N.Y. 10017

IN THE UNITED KINGDOM
PADDINGTON PRESS LTD
231 The Vale
London W3

IN CANADA
distributed by
RANDOM HOUSE OF CANADA LTD
5390 Ambler Drive
Mississauga
Ontario L4W 1Y7

TABLE OF CONTENTS

LIST OF ILLUSTRATIONS

PREFACE

"**W**HY WERE THERE no great women artists?" One of the purposes of this book is to demonstrate that this question —though still frequently asked with genuine concern and bewilderment—is moot. The question that should be asked, rather, is, "Why is so little known about great women artists of the past?" The answer to this would seem to point to a collective and, rather recent, cultural neglect. The basic art survey books used today only rarely allude to the names of women artists, and even most histories dealing with specific periods of art do not seriously consider their work. And yet in the past women were appointed as court painters, were accepted as professionals, and were unstintingly appreciated by their contemporaries. As late as the seventeenth century, accounts of women artists compared them proudly to such heroines of antiquity as Helena or Calypso. Since the Victorian age, named ironically after its female monarch, a conspiracy of silence seems to have descended upon male chroniclers, and while the history of art was developing into a respected and crowded discipline, historians have conspicuously, if perhaps unconsciously, overlooked or relegated to footnotes the accomplishments and even the existence of women artists. I hope that this book, by presenting a selection of outstanding women artists over the past five centuries, will constitute a beginning in a redress of balances.

A strikingly consistent fact which emerges from a study of the earliest known women artists of the Renaissance is that the reason they were allowed to develop their skills was because they were the daughters of artists. They were able to learn how to paint because of the availability of their own fathers' studios and training. What about the untapped talent of those potentially creative women whose fathers were not practicing artists? Sofonisba Anguissola, born of a noble family, is the only exception I have found so far in the sixteenth century; a few more appear for the seventeenth century: Judith Leyster in democratic Holland and Mary Beale of England.

daughter of a clergyman. In the age of Enlightenment, as women's social position improved, the chance for artistic instruction outside the family expanded as well, and more women studied to be artists through talent and inclination rather than because of family tradition. However, even during the nineteenth century it remained difficult for a woman to choose and pursue the profession of artist unless she came from a wealthy or artistically involved family. Edmonia Lewis and Suzanne Valadon are notable exceptions.

Another fact which surfaces from this study is that few women before the nineteenth century attempted sculpture. The legendary figure of Sabina von Steinbach is known to us for having completed the work of her father, Erwin, on Strasbourg Cathedral in the thirteenth century, and the shadowy figure of Properzia de' Rossi, carver of two marble reliefs for the church of San Petronio in Bologna, appears to be the only female sculptor to emerge during the Italian Renaissance. In seventeenth-century Spain Luisa Roldán achieved sufficient fame to be appointed court sculptor to Charles II. The breakthrough, however, occurred in the nineteenth century when Harriet Hosmer, Louisa Lander, Emma Stebbins, Margaret Foley, and other intrepid Americans traveled to Rome and managed to create names for themselves as neo-classical sculptors. Elisabet Ney made her successful artistic voyage in the opposite direction: after sculpting Bismarck, Schopenhauer, and King Ludwig II, she emigrated from Germany to Texas where she continued to do marble portraits of leading public figures and where she initiated art studies at the University of Texas and in the public schools of her adopted state. In modern times the roll call of women sculptors is impressive: Louise Nevelson, Barbara Hepworth, Mary Callery, Alicia Penalba, Sophie Täuber-Arp, Marisol, to name only a few.

Some of the women painters whose names are most familiar to the public are omitted from this book because of the desire to include lesser-known figures of equal merit. Mary Cassatt, for example, needs no further introduction. Berthe Morisot and Eva Gonzalès are mentioned in the literature on Impressionist art. Romaine Brooks was recently the subject of a retrospective exhibition with a comprehensive catalogue devoted to her work, and a monograph has just been published on Sonia Delauney. I regret being unable to include the magnificent paintings of Gabriele Münter and Marianne von Werekin, both of the Blue Rider movement in Germany. Since living women artists are coming into their own so encouragingly nowadays, this book has limited itself to artists of the past.

Perhaps this study will help to dispel some of the amusing and fallacious myths that have sprung up concerning women artists, such as that of the characteristic "female touch" and "female theme." In the same way that it is impossible to determine the sex of a writer by the individual's handwriting, there is, in general, no perceptible distinction between the touch of the male and female artist. Much of the art-historical literature facilely dismisses a work of fine detail as "obviously executed by a feminine hand," when in actuality it is as impossible to detect a sexual difference between the still lifes of Rachel Ruysch and Jan de Heem as it is to deduce a "feminine" touch in the powerful sculptures of Germaine Richier. As for women's reputed proclivity for the theme of *Mother and Child* or *Flowers*, the evidence in this book is that women excelled at portraiture and were undaunted by the same gamut of subjects undertaken by their male counterparts. Maria Sibylla Merian left the security of commercial Amsterdam in the seventeenth century to paint the exotic wildlife of South American jungles, Sofonisba Anguissola innovated a new type of group portraiture, the Venetian Rosalba Carriera introduced pastel portraits which became the vogue in Paris, Germaine Richier pioneered a bold, new expression in bronze sculpture, and I. Rice Pereira experimented in the third dimension by adding corrugated glass to her abstract paintings.

It is my hope that this book will serve as an introduction to the subject of these neglected women artists and that many monographs will follow. Should not someone study the work of Marietta Tintoretto and Levina Teerling? Why is there no book yet on Artemisia Gentileschi or Judith Leyster? It would be rewarding if the sensitive diary and letters of Paula Modersohn-Becker were translated into English. There are catalogues of the numerous exhibits of Richier's sculptures, but no one has ever written a probing monograph on her. The dearth of material on these artists has dictated that some of my chapters be necessarily stronger in biography, whereas others deal more with the oeuvre of the artist. This survey deals with only twenty-two women artists and yet covers an ambitious span of five centuries. It is thus with a sense of reluctance that the study ends here with such a numerically limited scope but also with a sense of gratification that for perhaps the first time a study has been encouraged in which women have been considered intrinsically as artists—rather than as artistic phenomena.

As our hidden heritage of women artists becomes more apparent and solidly annexed to the mainstream of history, we might look forward to the publication of monographs on the artists perused here and closer scrutiny of the contribution of all women artists throughout the centuries.

AUTHOR'S NOTE AND ACKNOWLEDGMENTS

Research for this book began in 1968 when I was in Europe gathering material for a doctoral dissertation on the Spanish painter Luis Meléndez. The sparkling richness of four still lifes hanging in the Prado Museum caught my eye and made me wonder who the unfamiliar seventeenth-century painter "Clara Peeters" might be. Then in Naples I was struck by the arresting quality of a *Self-Portrait* by a certain Sofonisba Anguissola, and I decided to begin a file on the then still-unusual topic of women artists. Since that time I have seen additional work by the Flemish painter Clara Peeters but have not included her in this book because more biographical research needs to be done in Belgian archives. On the other hand, I have been fortunate enough to pursue the subject of the Anguissola sisters in depth. My research has been aided by such people as Dr. Friderike Klauner of the Kunsthistorisches Museum in Vienna, Dr. Kurt Woisetschläger of the Graz Museum, and Dr. Xavier de Salas and Srta. Da. Rocio Arnaez of the Prado.

While teaching a seminar on women artists at Southern Methodist University in 1973, I was able to share my research with a very alert group of graduates and undergraduates who in turn engaged in fruitful investigation of several modern women artists.

I should like to express my appreciation to Southern Connecticut State College for granting me a leave of absence during the fall of 1972 to continue the research for this book in Europe, and to voice deep gratitude to my colleagues there for their moral support during the preparation of the manuscript. I acknowledge with pleasure the stimulating conversations on the subject of women artists with many of them as well as with Ms. Madeleine Fidell Beaufort, formerly of the Institute of Fine Arts, Professor Wayne Dynes of Columbia University, Professor Megan Laird Comini of Southern Methodist University, Professor Ann Harris of the State University of New York, Albany, Professor John R. Martin of Princeton University, Professor

Paula Harper of Stanford University, Ms. Sarah Schmidt of Yale University, and Dr. Priscilla Muller of the Hispanic Society of America.

My appreciation also goes to the gallery directors, private collectors, and museum curators who have assisted me in obtaining the photographs and permission to reproduce the works of art. In particular, I would like to thank Dr. Raffaello Causa of the Capodimonte Museum, Dr. Pierre Rosenberg of the Louvre, Dr. Kazimierz Malinowski of the Poznán Museum, Mr. Robert Kashey of the Shepherd Gallery, Mr. R. I. Frost of the Buffalo Bill Historical Center, Ms. Lynn Vermillion of the San Jose Public Library, Mr. and Mrs. S. M. Bebb of London, Ms. Emily Comer of the Virginia Museum of Fine Arts, Ms. Berthe Bülow-Jacobsen of the State Museum of Art, Copenhagen, Mme Tatiana Loguine-Mouraviev of Les Amis de Gontcharova/Larionov, Mr. Peter Bird of the Arts Council of Great Britain, and the National Gallery of Art, Washington.

Research for this book would not have been possible without the use of the Art Library at Yale University, the Frick Art Reference Library, Marguand Library of Princeton University, the Guggenheim Museum library, the Museum of Modern Art library, and the Print Room of the British Museum. My sincere thanks go to the helpful staff members of these institutions.

I am especially grateful to Professor Alessandra Comini of Columbia University who patiently read each chapter of the manuscript and offered so many valuable comments.

January 1974   Eleanor Tufts

New Haven, Connecticut

FIG. 1 SOFONISBA ANGUISSOLA, *Self-Portrait at the Spinet*

I SOFONISBA ANGUISSOLA
1535/40 · 1625

THE CITY OF CREMONA, famous for its violins since the sixteenth century, has given us another elegant product scarcely noted by history: Sofonisba Anguissola, the first distinguished woman painter of the Renaissance. At least fifty impressive paintings in museums and private collections all over the world are securely attributed to her.[1]

The eldest of *six* artist-sisters, Sofonisba was a child prodigy whose work attracted the attention of Michelangelo and Vasari. Michelangelo sent drawings to her which she reproduced in oil and returned to him for his comments.[2] Occasionally she gave him one of her own drawings, for example, *Boy Pinched by a Crayfish* (FIG. 2), which was eventually forwarded as a gift to the Florentine duke, Cosimo de' Medici. The work became so popular that other artists made copies of it, and it may well have inspired Caravaggio's famous *Boy Bitten by a Lizard*. What must have appealed to Michelangelo and the other artists, who admired this lively drawing (fortunately still preserved today), was the fact that a real-life incident, in which an older child comforts a little boy who cries out with pain and revulsion as a crayfish pinches his finger, had been so vividly caught by the quick hand of the artist.

Giorgio Vasari, the self-appointed biographer of Renaissance artists, who traveled up and down Italy gathering information and searching out works of art, visited the Anguissola family in 1566 and wrote as follows of Sofonisba's work:

> . . . I have this year seen a picture in her father's house at Cremona, most carefully finished, representing her three sisters playing at chess, in the company of an old lady of the house, making them appear alive and lacking speech only. In another she has portrayed her father between his daughter Minerva, distinguished in painting and letters, and his son Asdrubale, also breathing likenesses.[3]

21

The painting of the *Three Sisters Playing Chess* (FIG. 3) described by Vasari is recognized today as possibly the first of a new kind of portraiture showing the sitters engaged in a *genre* type of activity. We have already seen Sofonisba's particular eye for everyday events in *Boy Pinched by a Crayfish*.

For artistic instruction Sofonisba and Elena, the next oldest member of the family, studied three years with Bernardino Campi, a Mannerist painter of religious subjects and portraits. When he left Cremona for Milan in 1549, they continued their training with Bernardino Gatti, who came from the Parma circle of Correggio. We know little of Elena except that she entered a convent and was still living in 1584. Sofonisba's *Portrait of a Nun* (FIG. 4) is most probably a portrait of this sister Elena. We see the strong family resemblance in the long nose, arched brows, and large almond-shaped eyes.

The third daughter, Lucia, was also artistically gifted and, in fact, was a pupil of Sofonisba's, but she died prematurely in 1565 while still in her teens. Her portrait of *Pietro Maria, Doctor of Cremona* (FIG. 5) is signed on the arm of the chair: (*sic*) "Lucia Anguisola Amilcaris F. Adolescens. F" ("this work made by Lucia Anguisola, daughter of Amilcare") and was seen by Vasari during his visit.

We know little of Minerva except that she too died prematurely. Vasari writes of meeting another sister Europa who, though still a child, had already executed many portraits including one of her mother which was sent to Sofonisba in the Spanish court. He also mentions the little girl Anna who was following her sisters in her pursuit of art; one of her signed paintings, *The Holy Family with St. Francis*, can be seen today in the Cremona Pinacoteca.

The youngest child in the Anguissola family, Asdrubale, was a boy (born in 1551), and unlike his six artist-sisters he was not gifted artistically. Very possibly the elegant *Portrait of a Boy* (FIG. 6) in the Walters Art Gallery is of him. The boy does resemble Asdrubale who can be seen in a full-length portrait with his father, his sister Minerva, and a dog in the Hage Collection in Nivaagaard (Denmark). Although this handsome portrait of a boy dressed in black against a green background is merely attributed to Sofonisba, it corresponds convincingly to her style. It has the same linearism and studied positioning of the hands seen in her other portraits of children (the *Attavanti Boy and Girl*, Oberlin College; the *Gaddi Children*, Lord Methuen's Collection; and the *Three Sisters Playing Chess*, Poznán). Perhaps overwhelmed by his sisters' talents, little Asdrubale left no historical imprint.[4]

Sofonisba's reputation as a skilled portraitist was so great that news of her abilities extended beyond Italy, and in 1559 she was invited by King Philip II to come to the Spanish court. The following year, while still in her early twenties, Sofonisba arrived in Madrid and found it so to her liking that she remained for twenty years, working no longer as a prodigy but as a highly respected artist. Unfortunately, we know little of these years in Spain, but a *Portrait of Philip II* in the National Portrait Gallery, London, is attributed to her, and a *Portrait of the Queen* (Isabel of Valois) in the Kunsthistorisches Museum, Vienna (FIG. 7), is signed by her.[5] Documents exist concerning other royal portraits by her; for example, Pope Pius IV asked her to do a portrait of the Spanish queen for him. Sofonisba sent the following letter to accompany the completed work to Rome:

> Holy Father,
> I have learned from your Nuncio that you desired a portrait of my royal mistress by my hand. I considered it a singular favor to be allowed to serve your Holiness, and I asked Her Majesty's permission, which was readily granted, seeing the paternal affection which your Holiness displays to her. I have taken the opportunity of sending it by this knight. It will be a great pleasure to me if I have gratified your Holiness's wish, but I must add that, if the brush could represent the beauties of the queen's soul to your eyes, they would be marvelous. However, I have used the utmost diligence to present what art can show, to tell your Holiness the truth. And so I humbly kiss your most holy feet. Madrid, September 16, 1561.
> Your Holiness's most humble servant
> Sofonisba Anguisciola[6]

The Pope acknowledged the portrait with gifts and sent a personal note back to Sofonisba:

> *Pius Papa IV. Dilecta in Christa filia.* We have received the portrait of our dear daughter the Queen of Spain, which you have sent. It has given us the utmost satisfaction both for the person represented, whom we love like a father for the piety and the good qualities of her mind, and because it is well and diligently executed by your hand. We thank you and assure you that we shall treasure it among our choicest possessions, and commend your marvelous talent which is the least among your numerous qualities. And so we send you our benediction.
> May God save you.
> *Dat. Rome die 15 Octobris 1561.*[7]

Sofonisba also painted the Prince, Don Carlos, and a number of other portraits which were lost in the palace fire of the seventeenth century. It is quite possible that one day some of the surviving portraits of the royal children will be ascribed to Sofonisba, just as, most recently a scholar has given to her the original of two portraits of Queen Isabel which are known today only in copies by Juan Pantoja in the Prado Museum.[8]

In 1580 Sofonisba left Spain in order to marry a Sicilian, Don Fabrizio di Moncada, who took her to live in Palermo. Upon his death four years later, she decided to sail back to her homeland. As buoyant in her personal life as in her long distinguished career as a painter, Sofonisba was able to find love again, indeed rather quickly, for en route she fell in love with the ship's captain, a scion of the noble Lomellino family, whom she married at debarkation in Genoa. She apparently continued to visit Sicily occasionally because in 1624 the young Flemish painter, Anthony van Dyck, sketched her portrait as he paid his respects to her in Palermo This drawing in his Italian Sketchbook, preserved at Chatsworth House in England, is accompanied by the following inscription:

> Portrait of Signora Sophonisba, painter. Copied from life in Palermo on the 12th day of July of the year 1624, when she was 96 years of age, still of good memory, clear senses and kind. . . . While I painted her portrait, she gave me advice as to the light, which should not be directed from too high as not to cause too strong a shadow on her wrinkles, and many more good speeches, as well as telling me parts of her life-story, in which one could see that she was a wonderful painter after nature. . . .

There is new evidence to suggest that Van Dyck erred when he jotted down such a venerable age for the painter,[9] but at any rate the elderly Sofonisba did die the following year, and her grave in a Palermo church is marked by a memorial stone placed there by her mourning sea captain.

FIG. 2 SOFONISBA ANGUISSOLA, *Boy Pinched by a Crayfish*

FIG. 3 SOFONISBA ANGUISSOLA, *Three Sisters Playing Chess*

FIG. 4 SOFONISBA ANGUISSOLA, *Portrait of a Nun*

FIG. 5 LUCIA ANGUISSOLA, *Pietro Maria, Doctor of Cremona*

FIG. 6 SOFONISBA ANGUISSOLA, *Portrait of a Boy*

FIG. 7 SOFONISBA ANGUISSOLA, *Portrait of Queen Isabel*

FIG. 8 LAVINIA FONTANA, *Self-Portrait*, 1579

2 LAVINIA FONTANA
1552·1614

No FEWER THAN TWENTY-THREE women painters were recorded as active in the city of Bologna during the sixteenth and seventeenth centuries by Luigi Crespi in his book *Vite de' Pittori Bolognesi* of 1769. Bologna was accustomed to educated women, for its university actually permited women as lecturers in the classrooms. Many became famous for their scholarship and instruction in law, and one of them, Novella d'Andrea, apparently a striking beauty, is reputed to have found it necessary to lecture from behind a large screen to avoid distracting the students with her personal charms.

The first of Bologna's numerous women painters to achieve renown throughout Italy was Lavinia Fontana, whose *Self-Portrait Seated at her Desk* (FIG. 8) shows her as an art collector and connoisseur of antiquity. Lavinia had ample opportunity to indulge her hobby, for, as one of the most successful portrait artists of the day, she was honored by popes and aristocracy not only with commissions but with valuable gifts.

Born in 1552, Lavinia was taught to paint by her father, Prospero, active in Bologna as both an artist and a teacher. Among her fellow students were Ludovico Carracci—older cousin of Agostino and Annibale—and a young man named Gian Paolo Zappi from Imola. It was this latter colleague, Zappi, who was to claim Lavinia's hand in marriage and who gave up his own career to care for their family and to paint many of the frames for his wife's pictures.

Lavinia became enormously popular with the leading families of Bologna who were delighted by her sophisticated colors and her ability to paint in detail their fine clothes and jewelry. A contemporary chronicler, Baglione, noted with only a bit of wonder, "Even though Lavinia was a women, she did extremely well for herself in this type of painting."[1]

Her important group portrait of the Gozzadini Family (FIG. 9) was used as an illustration by Litta in his *Famiglie Celebri Italiane* (1839). Old Senator

Gozzadini is shown seated and flanked on either side by his two daughters and their husbands. The daughters were married to brothers, which explains the look-alike appearance of the spouses. The brocades and jewels worn by the women are rendered with glittering brilliance. The opening up of space through the device of a view into a distant hall or room is repeated by Fontana in a number of her male portraits, for example, the great Lenten preacher, *Fra Panigarola* (Uffizi, Florence), *Francesco dal Pero* (Dal Pero Collection, Imola), and *Carlo Sigonia* (Museo Communale, Modena)—an interesting twist to the contemporary School of Fountainbleau's fondness for combining the view into the distance with the close-up motif of a woman at her toilette.

Lavinia also created her own distinctive formula for female sitters: they are shown seated in an armchair and with one hand they caress a—usually alert—lap dog. The Walters Art Gallery owns one of these portraits (FIG. 10); among others are the *Portrait of the Lady of the Ruina House* (Galleria Pitti, Florence) and *Portrait of Constanza Alidosi* (Collection of Dr. F. Kung, New York). In these works the richness of detail is matched by a profundity of characterization that justifies Lavinia's fame as a portraitist.

One of her most ambitious paintings is *The Visit of the Queen of Sheba* (FIG. 11), which sparkles since the removal of repaints. The queen is accompanied by a bevy of splendidly gowned attendants, many of whom focus their attention on the servant who enters at the right bearing a tray laden with golden objects. A red-jacketed dwarf gestures toward the approaching servant and the glistening gifts. Meanwhile at the left Sheba kneels on a red carpet in homage to Solomon who rises from his canopied throne. Behind the visitors is a view of a distant landscape seen over a low balustrade, very similar to the background which Lavinia includes in her *Minerva* painting in the Galleria Borghese (Rome).

This scene has long been reputed to represent the Duke and Duchess of Mantua and members of their court. The ruling ducal family during the Renaissance were the Gonzagas, known for their lavish patronage of the arts. The particular duke and duchess at this time must have been Vincenzo I, who lived 1562 to 1612 (almost exactly contemporary with Lavinia), and Leonora de' Medici. Vincenzo traveled a great deal, sometimes with a cortège of as many as 2000 people, so Lavinia may not have needed to make a trip to Mantua to carry out this commission. In fact, in 1600 the duke and duchess went to Florence for the wedding of Maria de' Medici, and they may well have passed through Bologna.

Certainly the Queen of Sheba looks very much like Leonora as we see her portrayed by Rubens in his painting of the *Trinity Adored by the Gonzaga*

Family, while the features of Solomon correspond convincingly to those of Vincenzo I on a contemporary coin depicting his profile.

It is known that Vicenzo obtained the poet Torquato Tasso's release from the hospital of St. Anne, and it is thus perhaps essential to Lavinia's depiction of the Duke and Duchess of Mantua as Solomon and Sheba to mention that in the famous discourse on Feminine Virtue, which Tasso dedicated to Vincenzo's mother in 1582, the poet says that women who do not seek love out of unbridled desire should be praised like Sheba who came to Solomon. Another reason that the analogy to Solomon may have appealed especially to the Gonzagas is that they treasured in their art collection an onyx vessel believed to be a relic from the Temple of Solomon. (A pictorial precedent for lending the features of a ruling monarch to the Old Testament figure of Solomon is Holbein's miniature of *Solomon and the Queen of Sheba*, in which the indefatigable Henry VIII welcomes yet another queen to his court).

The presence of the dwarf in this painting reminds one of the continuing interest in dwarfs at the Mantuan court. They are seen in the famous frescoes which Mantegna painted on the walls of the palace in the fifteenth century, and, when the Gonzaga finances dwindled early in the seventeenth century because of the failure of the silk industry, a duke who succeeded Vincenzo, prefered to buy one more dwarf—then on the market in Hungary—than to prevent the pending sale of the Gonzaga art collection to the English king.[2]

Seventeenth-century and more recent biographers[3] usually refer to Lavinia as palatine painter to Gregory XIII, and indeed it is true that she was personally acquainted with her fellow Bolognese. But while it may have been Pope Gregory who encouraged her to take her talents to Rome, it was not until the papacy of Clement VIII that Fontana actually transfered her family to the Holy City. There had been serious illness in her immediate family that impeded her departure. One of her daughters was blinded by an accident, several of her children did not survive infancy, and she was further detained in Bologna by having to care for her very frail father who died in 1597. In about 1603 she finally was able to leave her native city and to move southward with her entire household including her octogenarian mother.

Her husband and a son had already preceded her to Rome as had her painting, *The Virgin and S. Giacinto*, commissioned by Cardinal Ascoli. Baglione writes that the successful reception of this work had created a clamor for the artist in Rome. One of Lavinia's largest commissions upon arrival was an altarpiece for St. Paul's Outside the Walls, an over-lifesize *Stoning of St. Stephen*. Romeo Galli in his short monograph on the artist quotes a letter of 1604 in which extra space is begged from the Cardinal d'Este in order that Lavinia might more comfortably work upon the huge painting. The altarpiece was, unfortunately, destroyed in the 1823 fire of the basilica.

In a city of important and self-important people, Fontana was incessantly in demand as a portraitist. As Galli writes, "she painted the image of Pope Paul V destined for a king of Persia, portraits of ambassadors, of princes, of cardinals."[4] Mancini, her contemporary, in his *Viaggio di Roma* specifically mentions seeing Lavinia's portrait of the Persian ambassador which hung in the Castello di Sant' Angelo.

Among her extant Roman paintings are a number of double portraits, such as that of *Monsignor Ratta with a Young Cleric* (FIG. 12). It is an impressive work, not without psychological depth and one which reminds the modern beholder of Raphael's earlier *Portrait of Pope Leo and his Nephews*.

One of Lavinia's most imposing religious paintings is *The Holy Family with Infant John the Baptist*, which serves as the altarpiece in the Pantheon of the Infantes in The Escorial. The Spanish Baroque artist and writer, Francisco Pacheo, records that Philip II paid Lavinia 1000 ducados for the work,[5] and another seventeenth-century account[6] describes the painting as already in place in the chapel, where, despite the sepulchral gloom, the magnificent colors and buoyant composition may still be appreciated today.

Many of her religious paintings are in the churches and the museum of her native city. *The Birth of Mary*, a large painting shot through with chiaroscuro effects, hangs in the Church of the Trinity. Light flickers dramatically upon various narrative episodes which climb in a zig-zag fashion from the crowded bottom of this composition to the ring of watching angels at the top. Another formidable work, *Queen Luisa of France Presenting her Son Francis I to S. Francesco di Paolo* (FIG. 13), is replete with fashionably coiffeured ladies, running servants, attentive soldiers, and enthusiastic trumpeters, all of whom, nevertheless, do not in the slightest ruffle the saint's composure. Other religious paintings by Lavinia hang in the museums of Dresden, Naples, Leningrad, and Stockholm.

Lavinia Fontana's reputation continued to grow at home as well as abroad, and in 1611, a few years before her death, a portrait medal was cast in her honor (FIG. 14). Whereas the coin face presents us with a very respectable and classical Roman matron, the verso showing the artist inspired and at work—her hair in a frenzy—is perhaps more appropriate for Fontana in view of her truly prodigious output: 135 documented works[7] and eleven pregnancies before her death in 1614 at the age of sixty-two.

FIG. 9 LAVINIA FONTANA, *Gozzadini Family*, 1584

FIG. 10 LAVINIA FONTANA, *Lady with a Lap Dog*

FIG. 11 LAVINIA FONTANA, *The Visit of the Queen of Sheba*

FIG. 12 LAVINIA FONTANA, *Monsignor Ratta with a Young Cleric*

FIG. 13 LAVINIA FONTANA, *Queen Luisa of France Presenting her Son Francis I to S. Francesco di Paolo*, 1590

FIG. 14a *Portrait Medal of Lavinia Fontana*, recto

FIG. 14b *Portrait Medal of Lavinia Fontana,* verso

FIG. 15 LEVINA TEERLING, *Self-Portrait* (age: 50)

3 LEVINA TEERLING
c1515·1576

IN THE SIXTEENTH CENTURY Levina Teerling was an undisputed and international celebrity. Yet at the present time few works are positively attributed to her hand. This Flemish painter was sufficiently well known to be invited to England by King Henry VIII, and, according to official records, she was paid a higher salary than Holbein.[1] Perhaps more impressive, however, is the fact that she was retained as court painter by the three successive monarchs: Edward VI, Mary I, and Elizabeth I.

Teerling's specialty was miniatures, and due to their extreme popularity as articles of dress in England, not only she, but several other Flemish artists, such as Katherine Maynors, Alice Carmillion, Ann Smiter, and the entire Horebout family,[2] were imported to meet the demands of a voracious miniature-loving public. Even Queen Elizabeth is reported to have snatched a portrait of young Cecil from Lady Derby's bosom and tied it to her shoe.

The date of Levina's birth is not known. She was the eldest of five daughters (her mother died in 1542) and followed the profession of her father, Simon Bening, and of her grandfather, Alexander Bening, both famous miniaturists. One of her sisters, Alexandra, remained close to the family profession by becoming an art dealer.

The Bening sisters were not alone in realizing careers in sixteenth-century Flanders, for in their early teens the daughters of Christophe Plantin, the printer of the first Polyglot Bible, were managing a business in Antwerp.[3] They were associated with the family's lingerie and lace shop and were entrusted with purchasing and with hiring employees. Catherine Plantin began at the age of eleven to write up the accounts of her workers, and three years later she was sent to Malines to negotiate with the lace-makers there. Another daughter, Martine, by the age of fifteen was already the employer of thirty-five workers in three different cities, providing them with cloth as well as objects to decorate. Guicciardini in his *Description de tout le Pays-Bas* in 1567 wrote that the business-minded Plantin sisters were not unique, but that many Flemish women were active in commerce and were fluent in several languages, some in as many as six different tongues.

Levina studied in Bruges with her father, and one of the earliest works in which her hand is detected is the *Hennessy Hours*, which her father illuminated about 1530. Levina is credited with a spirited and crowded scene of *Christ Before Pilate* (FIG. 16) as well as with other pages in this work.[4]

The artist married George Teerling, and after they settled the estate of her father-in-law in 1545,[5] the couple left for England in response to the flattering summons of Henry VIII. By January 1546 her name already appeared as the "King's paintrix" in the Exchequer's accounts. Later a reference is made to a small picture of the Trinity which she gave to Queen Mary as a New Year's gift, and subsequent entries in those accounts refer to paintings presented to Queen Elizabeth, such as Her Majesty's portrait finely executed on a card, and, in 1561, the Queen and other courtiers depicted together in a miniature on a box.

One of the rare miniatures securely ascribed to Levina is the so-called *Portrait of Lady Hunsdon*, dated 1575, in the Rijksmuseum (FIG. 19). The lady's dress is black with an embroidered design on her white sleeves. The background is a pure ultramarine, which was the customary color used to set off the portrait head in miniatures. In the other portraits attributed to Levina, such as the one in a circular ivory box, formerly in the J. Pierpont Morgan collection, and another in the Victoria and Albert Museum, we see the extravagant attention of a former manuscript illustrator applied to details of costume and coiffeur. Up until about 1950 a locket containing a pair of miniatures in the Victoria and Albert Museum was thought to be by her, but today these two portraits of little girls are attributed to the English miniaturist Isaac Oliver. Writers in the past have for cogent reasons assumed this pair to be by Teerling, but in recent years the Oliver scholars have been more active in establishing his body of work and by their zeal have cast Levina into even greater obscurity.

Teerling was not limited to single images in her miniatures, but also did group scenes such as the *Maundy* of 1572 (Earl of Beauchamp Collection) which was presented to the last monarch whom she served, Queen Elizabeth I. In the foreground Elizabeth, garbed in blue, is seen advancing to perform the ceremony of the washing of the feet while a spirited throng of brightly dressed ladies and courtiers eagerly surrounds her.

Very few portraits of Elizabeth as princess are known. In fact, the Queen showed an unusual reluctance to pose throughout her life and apparently sat for only five artists, including Levina. The life-size *Portrait of Elizabeth as Princess* in Windsor Castle (FIG. 20) has been attributed to Levina, and in it

44

we see her prowess of characterization in capturing the alert gaze of an impatient sovereign. In this three-quarter length portrait the Princess is magnificently dressed in carmine red and already shows her penchant for wearing an excessive array of jewelry. A payment to Levina of £10 in 1551 may refer to this painting or to an interesting miniature of the young Elizabeth (FIG. 18) in which the sitter is again portrayed looking purposefully forward in a direct confrontation with the viewer.

The royal accounts indicate that Levina was highly respected in the English court. She enjoyed the status of a "gentlewoman" and received numerous gifts from the four monarchs whom she served together with an annuity for life. She, along with her husband and son, Marcus, all received English citizenship in 1566, and ten years later, it is reported, she died in their home in Stepney.

FIG. 16 LEVINA TEERLING, "Christ Before Pilate," Ms. II 158, fol. 70 v., *Les Heures de Notre Dame*

FIG. 17 LEVINA TEERLING, *Portrait of a Girl*, 1549

FIG. 18 Attributed to Levina Teerling, *Miniature of Elizabeth I as Princess*

FIG. 19 LEVINA TEERLING, *Portrait of Lady Hunsdon, 1575*

FIG. 20 Attributed to Levina Teerling, *Elizabeth I as Princess*

FIG. 21 CATHARINA VAN HEMESSEN, *Self-Portrait*, 1548

4 CATHARINA VAN HEMESSEN
1528 · after 1587

Low MANY PEOPLE today know Catharina van Hemessen? Perhaps at the most, a handful, Yet, in the sixteenth century Catharina was recognized as a talented portraitist in her native land, Flanders, and was honored by a royal invitation to Spain. Her many commissioned portraits hang in museums in London, Barnard Castle, Cambridge, England; Amsterdam, Brussels, Antwerp, and Providence, Rhode Island.

A *Self-Portrait* in the Basle Museum (FIG. 21) is signed "Ego Caterina de Hemessen me pinxi 1548" ("I, Caterina de Hemessen, painted myself in 1548"), and she further designates her age "20" on the panel. Seated at her easel, she portrays herself at work, in the act of sketching a head onto a small wooden panel, while holding a palette and brushes in her left hand. It is interesting for us to be able to observe in this self-portrait exactly *how* the artist worked, using a "mahl" (painting) stick to steady her hand and beginning her portrait, not with an outline of the entire composition, but with a scrupulous delineation of the facial features. Our artist is clothed for the cold northern climate in a high-necked black dress with red velvet sleeves, pink lace collar and cuffs, and a white coif over her brown hair. The expression on her face is intense and suggests a serious dedication to the painter's craft.

From this same year is another painting by Catharina, which writers over the years have presumed to be a self-portrait. This picture in the Cologne Museum (FIG. 22) shows a young girl playing a spinet, and the age of the sitter is recorded on the panel as "22". The artist and the spinet-player wear dresses that are almost identical, and there is a strong facial resemblance between them—with large eyes dominating a moon-shaped face—but Catharina's hair comes to a point, forming a widow's peak, and her eyebrows are not as evenly defined as the spinet-player's. It seems logical to suggest that the musician, who was twenty-two the same year that Catharina records her own age as twenty, is the artist's older sister, Christina who was the first-born daughter of their painter-father, Jan Sanders van Hemessen.

51

A fact which emerges from the study of women artists in the Renaissance is that the reason a woman was able to learn how to paint was that her father was, almost invariably, an artist. Thus, the availability of the father's studio and his training is what made it possible for a woman to realize her artistic potentiality. Sofonisba Anguissola, being of a noble Italian family to whom instruction in the arts were part of a general upbringing, is a notable exception.

When Catharina was born in Antwerp in 1528, Flanders was ruled by Spain, and Antwerp itself was both a thriving commercial port and a stimulating international center. When a ruler of the Spanish royal family sailed to Flanders from Spain, Antwerp was the port of entry, and the city continued to be an attractive cultural magnet for another hundred years. In 1609 Rubens requested permission from the Archduchess Isabella Clara Eugenia, whom he served, to maintain his home and studio in Antwerp instead of Brussels, the seat of government.

As Catharina became more practiced, she collaborated with her father on such famous paintings as his *Joyful Company* (Karlsruhe Museum), in which we may safely presume that many of the background episodes were added by Catharina's hand.[1] Several prominent scholars of Flemish painting today are beginning to speculate that the genre painter known only as the "Monogrammist of Brunswick" may indeed be either Catharina van Hemessen or Mayken Verhulst, another woman painter of the sixteenth century who has been overlooked but is known to have been the first teacher of her grandson, Jan "Velvet" Brueghel.

Two signed religious paintings by Catharina are *The Rest on the Flight into Egypt* (private collection, Mons) and *Christ and Veronica* (FIG. 23). The former, dated 1555, is large and very close in style to her father's compositions such as his *Holy Family* (Stockholm) in which powerful figures dominate a detailed landscape. Catharina's *Christ and Veronica* is of a smaller size and its greater meticulousness and crowded composition recall her preference for working in a small-scale format as indicated in the *Self-Portrait* of 1548.

It is in her portraits that Catharina displays a truly outstanding mastery of characterization. In the reserve collection (in the basement) of the National Gallery, London, one can see an undeniably impressive male portrait of 1552 (FIG. 24) and a female portrait (FIG. 25) which, while physically smaller, is certainly a substantial work with spectacular highlights on the red sleeves and with a distinctive particularization of the sad, wan face.

In a pair of portraits in the Museum of Fine Arts in Brussels a fine line of light catches the edge of the sitters' clothing and distinguishes them from the background. With her customary precision van Hemessen clearly imprints onto the panel her name and date of the painting and the ages of the sitters, probably a husband and wife. Another firmly dated and signed portrait in the Fitzwilliam Museum (Cambridge, England) shows an elderly woman of serious mien and dignified bearing. The Rijksmuseum *Portrait of a Lady* and the *Portrait of a Man* in the Museum of the Rhode Island School of Design both show slim-waisted, somber-eyed figures against dark, neutral backgrounds. Catharina's sympathetic, quiet style of portraiture can be characterized as follows: half-length figures with earnest expressions are shown in brightly colored garments against a dark background while their pale, white faces turn slightly away from the beholder—suggesting an intimate world upon which neither artist nor spectator really intrudes.

Perhaps we can assume that as the daughter of the popular and accomplished painter, Jan Sanders van Hemessen, Catharina had social as well as professional access to the good homes of Antwerp, for in 1554 Catharina married Chrétien de Morien, organist of Antwerp's cathedral. To meet someone in such a high position, our artist apparently moved with ease in an upper-class society, and indeed this is reflected in the appearance of her sitters as dignified and well-to-do patricians.

Catharina enjoyed the royal patronage of Queen Mary of Hungary, Regent of the Low Countries, where she governed on behalf of her brother, the Spanish King Charles I, who controlled much of Europe as Holy Roman Emperor. When the Queen abdicated her regency in 1556, she invited Catharina and her husband to accompany her to Spain. The Royal Inventories of Furnishings that belonged to the Spanish royal family contain numerous references to Queen Mary's books of music and musical instruments, including several organs, and undoubtedly Catharina's husband was as well occupied with musical duties as was Catharina before her artist's easel. The paintings in the inventory of this period (the time of Philip II) do not specify artists' names and so we unfortunately lack documentary evidence of Catharina's activity in Spain. However, it is likely that she continued to paint portraits and religious compositions. Upon her death, Queen Mary left the talented couple a generous pension, and this enabled them to return and live out their days in their beloved Antwerp, where Catharina died sometime after 1587.

FIG. 22 CATHARINA VAN HEMESSEN, *Girl at the Spinet*, 1548

FIG. 23 CATHARINA VAN HEMESSEN, *Christ and Veronica*

FIG. 24 CATHARINA VAN HEMESSEN, *Portrait of a Man,* 1552

FIG. 25 CATHARINA VAN HEMESSEN, *Portrait of a Woman*, 1551

FIG. 26 ARTEMISIA GENTILESCHI, *Self-Portrait as 'La Pittura.'*

5 ARTEMISIA GENTILESCHI
1593 · c1652

Considered by many to be the greatest of Italian women artists, Artemisia Gentileschi earned her living as a painter in Rome, Florence, Genoa, Naples, and London.[1] Among her patrons were the Barberini family of Rome, the Grand Duke of Tuscany, the antiquarian scholar Cassiano dal Pozzo, Prince Ruffo of Sicily, the Spanish Duke of Alcalá, and the Royal Family of England. Art historians regard her as an especially important influence on the development of the Neapolitan school of painting—second only to Caravaggio in her impact—and she is also considered important for the French Baroque painter Simon Vouet[2] whose formulative years were spent in the same Italian cities in which Artemisia was active.

At first a student and protégé of her painter-father, Orazio, in Rome, Artemisia soon became known for her own colorful personality. Seventeenth-century biographers praised her as a brilliant conversationalist and a witty epigrammatist. Her private life was full of amorous affairs, and she became, not surprisingly, a superb writer of love letters. Nevertheless her first introduction to the ways of love and desire was as the victim of rape. While still a teen-ager, she was, as her father wrote in a petition to the Pope, "deflowered by force and known in the flesh many a time by Agostino Tasso, painter, close friend and colleague of the petitioner."[3] In a Roman court, on 18 March 1612, she supplied the information that during the previous year, when one day she found herself alone in the studio with her father's friend, the rape occured in spite of spirited resistance and even the infliction of wounds upon her attacker. She was later cross-examined—*under torture*—but never wavered in her testimony. Other witnesses, including Tasso's own sister, appeared in court to attest to his lustful, villainous ways. The upshot of the trial was that Tasso was sent to prison for over eight months while on 29 November 1612 Artemisia, at the age of nineteen, was married to a Florentine who spirited her away immediately to his native city.

Once in Florence Artemisia became well-known as an artist, and·by the time she was twenty-three she was made a member of the Academy—a most unusual honor for a women. One of her earliest subjects, and one which she treated several times, was the Old Testament (Apocrypha) story of Judith decapitating the Assyrian general Holofernes. In the light of Artemisia's personal history, it is certainly tempting to read a psychological interpretation into her attraction for this theme. Her earliest extant painting of this subject in the Galleria Pitti (FIG. 27) shows the deed already done: Holofernes's head is crammed into a basket, and Judith and her maidservant are listening warily for possible intruders. Both Artemisia and her father were impressed with the dramatic, shadowy paintings of Caravaggio, and in this work we see such Caravaggesque characteristics as three-quarter-length, animated figures, which inhabit the immediate foreground and fill the picture surface against a dark ("tenebrist") background. Judith, dressed in dark red, and the maid in bright yellow, appear to be contemporary women, not idealized Biblical figures, and are thus strongly reminiscent of the new, modern style with which Caravaggio had revolutionized painting in the classical ambience of Rome.

In a second version of this subject (FIG. 28), which Artemisia painted in Florence, she gives more expressive vent to her feelings. A buxom Judith is portrayed in the very act of decapitating Holofernes. One hand tightly clasps the warrior's hair, while with the other she determinedly cuts through his neck, sending the blood gushing upward as well as across the bed. The figures, which are now full-length, continue to be Caravaggesque in their frank naturalism.

The Detroit Institute of Art owns a later treatment of the same theme which Gentileschi painted about 1625 when she was back in Rome (FIG. 29). In this well-constructed painting Judith holds her hand against the candlelight to guard against discovery from outside the tent, while the maid stealthily wraps up the severed, bloody head. Judith's yellow dress, reflecting the red of the tent, is at the center of the composition between a green table and a purple and green-blue dress worn by the kneeling maid.

By this time Artemisia was well respected socially as well as professionally in Rome. She lived on the fashionable Via del Corso, and the records of her parish church, Sta. Maria del Popolo, indicate that already in 1625 she was designated godmother to a child named after her, and the following year to a child named after her daughter Prudentia.

The next decade of the 1630's finds our peripatetic artist living in Spanish-ruled Naples where she executed commissions for the "Empress"[4] and other wealthy clients in a new comfortable studio. Here she painted *The Birth of*

John the Baptist (FIG. 30), which was shipped to Spain along with other scenes from the life of St. John by the painter Massimo Stanzione. In this large work the spaciousness of the interior which the figures inhabit has been increased and emphasized, and a view has been opened up through an archway to blue sky—a device which may well have served as an inspiration for the famous Spanish painter, Jusepe Ribera, who was active in Naples at this time and intermittently at work on his painting, *The Institution of the Holy Eucharist*, finished in 1651.

Meanwhile, in her personal life Artemisia had long lost touch with her husband (by whom she had had at least one daughter), but not with her painter-father who was now in England, attempting, despite ill health, to carry out important commissions for King Charles I. Artemisia undertook the arduous trip from Naples to join her father around 1638 and even made her own contributions to the nine canvases being set into the ceiling of the Queen's House at Greenwich. She remained in England after Orazio's death, and from this period comes the famous *Self-Portrait as 'La Pittura'*, still in the Royal Collection at Hampton Court (FIG. 26). Since it has been pointed out that Artemisia follows the prescribed imagery for the allegorical figure of "Painting" as described by the sixteenth-century Cesare Ripa in his popular handbook on images, *Iconologia*, let us consider for a moment Ripa's words. He writes that the personification of "Painting" wears around her neck a chain from which hangs a mask, while at her feet lie a palette and brushes. He explains that the mask is an imitation of a human face, just as painting is an imitation of life. More interesting than the fact that we see all these attributes in Artemisia's self-portrait is that Ripa speaks of the golden chain "as a symbol of the continuity and interlocking nature of painting, each man learning from his master and continuing his master's achievements in the next generation." Therefore, it would seem to be no accident that Artemisia did her own portrait in this symbolic way at this time—as a memorial to her recently deceased master, her father. She has portrayed herself wearing a green dress which reflects mauve shadows. The sleeve of her right arm is pushed up as she energetically pursues her craft, and on the table she has inscribed her initials for us long to remember her as a "Gentileschi" rather than by her married name.

According to her contemporary biographers,[5] Gentileschi did many portraits, but very few are known today. One of the persons to whom she promised a self-portrait was Don Antonio Ruffo of Messina, famed for his commissioning Rembrandt and Guercino to do paintings of philosophers. She also told Ruffo she would send him works by her daughter who was carrying on the family tradition of painting into a third generation.

It was Naples to which Artemisia returned to resume her career. She continued to choose as her subjects heroic women of the Old Testament: Esther, famous for her courageous intercession on behalf of the Jewish people; Bathsheba, known for her dilemma in having to choose between fidelity to her husband or to her king; and Susanna, the beautiful wife of the Babylonian citizen whose garden was invaded by two lecherous elders whose advances she repelled. Particularly in Artemisia's choice of Susanna one detects the artist's personal identification with a beleaguered heroine of antiquity.

In the eighteenth century an enthusiastic collector of works by Artemisia was Graf Aloys Thomas Harrach who, during the brief time that the Austrians wrested the Kingdom of Naples from Spain, functioned as Viceroy. One of the paintings which he took back with him to Vienna was Artemisia's portrayal of *Esther and Ahasuerus* (recently acquired by the Metropolitan Museum). The Biblical account informs us that Queen Esther, a beautiful young Jewish woman who was married to the Persian king Ahasuerus, saved her people from slaughter in her husband's empire. The moment depicted in the painting (FIG. 31) is that when the Queen appears before the King to submit her petition; we see that Artemisia dramatically portrays Esther who falls back, swooning into the arms of two attendants, while a sympathetic Ahasuerus starts to rise from his throne to aid his stricken wife. The two protagonists are richly dressed: Esther in a vivid gold dress with brocade sleeves and a blue sash, and the dapper Ahasuerus in a black and white doublet over which is draped a crimson mantle.

In her late style Gentileschi moved away from her earlier Caravaggesque manner, which had gone out of fashion and been supplanted by the ever-recuring taste for classicism. We see this in her paintings of Bathsheba, such as the one in the Columbus, Ohio, Gallery of Arts (FIG. 32). Her figures are smaller in relation to the entire picture space, they are classically draped, and they are no longer individualistic, contemporary women but have idealized, perfect facial features. Furthermore, the artist's workshop was so well established by now that she was able to follow the tradition of hiring assistants to carry out the background accessories in her larger canvases. But the familiar hand of Artemisia is seen in the servant who bends over the silver bowl, recalling a similar kneeling figure in her *Birth of John the Baptist*, and her colors continue to be radiant: a dark blue dress on the kneeling maid, a maroon gown on the attendant who combs Bathsheba's hair, a pink drape over Bathsheba's lap, and a yellow dress with a transparent blue shawl on the attendant who holds out a plate of jewelry for her mistress's selection.

The exact circumstances and date of Artemisia's death are not known, but apparently she was still active as a painter when she died in her fifties. It is surprising that despite all the recognition given to her paintings and to her influence on the new generation of painters in Naples (Stanzione and Bernardo Cavallino), no book has ever been written on this major artist of the seventeenth century, who was proud to sign her work as a "Gentileschi."

FIG. 27 ARTEMISIA GENTILESCHI, *Judith with her Maidservant*

FIG. 28 ARTEMISIA GENTILESCHI, *Judith Decapitating Holofernes*

FIG. 29 ARTEMISIA GENTILESCHI, *Judith and Maidservant with the Head of Holofernes*

FIG. 30 ARTEMISIA GENTILESCHI, *The Birth of St. John the Baptist*

FIG. 31 ARTEMISIA GENTILESCHI, *Esther and Ahasuerus*

FIG. 32 ARTEMISIA GENTILESCHI, *David and Bathsheba*

FIG. 33 JUDITH LEYSTER, *Self-Portrait*

6 JUDITH LEYSTER
1609·1660

IN THE NATIONAL GALLERY at Washington an engaging self-portrait of the artist before the easel is prominently displayed. The beholder's attention is not only caught by the sex of the artist —female—but by the infectious *joie-de-vivre* expressed with such apparent ease in this picture. We see a slim-waisted young woman whose regular features, although not beautiful, are commanding in their communication of candid self-assertion and obvious enjoyment of craft. The painter's lips are parted, and, although dressed in her formal best with the stiff, starched collar of the times, she seems almost to lounge against her chair as she holds both her palette and brush with elegant ease. She wears a red skirt and black bodice, while the figure of the violinist in her canvas is gaily garbed in blue. The animation of both figures is immediately conveyed; the artist's mouth is open in a slight smile and the musician's face lights up with a laugh. We are looking at probably the best-known female painter of the seventeenth century, the Dutchwoman Judith Leyster whose lively scenes of everyday life—*genre* scenes—hang in the leading museums of Europe.

Here we have a painter whose father was not an artist. Jan Willemsz was a brewer who apparently took his surname from his Haarlem brewery, the "Ley-ster(re)." When his daughter signed her paintings, she used a monogram of JL plus a star, which was a play on the word "Ley/sterre," meaning lodestar.

Born in Haarlem in 1609, Judith was an exceptional child whose artistic talents were noted by the poet Samuel Ampzingh in his history of the city written in 1627. No information has been found regarding her earliest instruction; nevertheless, Leyster is interesting proof that in republican Holland it actually was possible for a girl born into a bourgeois family to receive artistic training, so that she, like her later compatriot painter, Jan Steen, whose father was also a brewer, could realize her potential as an artist. She was not the only women painter in Holland in the seventeenth century;

Maria van Oosterwyck was specializing in flower-pieces, other women are shown working as artists in the paintings of Metsu, and in nearby Flanders Clara Peeters was making a name for herself as a painter of fascinating still lifes.

In 1628, when she was nineteen, Leyster's family moved to the vicinity of Utrecht, where there was a flourishing school of artists, including Terbrugghen and Honthorst, who had just returned from Italy and who were impressed with Caravaggism—that style which had so strongly influenced Artemisia Gentileschi. The following year the Leyster family returned to the Haarlem area, and Judith presumably became a pupil of the city's leading artist, the famous Frans Hals. She was so warmly accepted into the painter's family that she served as a witness at the baptism of one of his children in 1631.

The esteem with which Leyster was soon held in her native city is evidenced by the fact that she was admited into the painter's guild, the Guild of St. Luke, at Haarlem in 1633. The records indicate that, by 1635, she was respected enough to have three pupils studying with her. At this time her amicable relations with Hals ended when she sued him for accepting an apprentice who had deserted her studio.

A major change occured in her personal life when at the age of twenty-seven, in 1636, she married a fellow painter, Jan Miense Molenaer. His work, although also specializing in genre scenes, is characterized by a greater number of figures in one composition and a more explicit delineation of background accessories. Leyster continues under the influence of her own master, Hals, employing a freer brushstroke in which the verve of the figure itself is emphasized and in which detail is suggested with a flickering stroke rather than minutely articulated. The married couple moved to the thriving port city of Amsterdam in the next year—possibly in search of patrons among the rich burgher class. Rembrandt too had moved from his native city to Amsterdam in the 1630's. Although Leyster gave birth to at least one son, she continued to paint and to use her maiden name in her signatures, but her household duties kept her busy and there was a noticeable decline in her artistic output.

Some of Leyster's paintings of single figures remind viewers of the work of Frans Hals in their capturing of a momentary spontaneity. However, in works such as *The Flute Player* (FIG. 35), there is considerable originality and freshness in her approach. The boy, dressed in a brownish-green jacket, purple trousers, and a bright red cap, plays his flute intently—introducing the idea of self-absorption. The painter's versatility and control of realism is demonstrated in the renditions of several musical instruments, and something as humble as the back wall is made more interesting by nuances of light, tone, and texture.

In her compositions involving more than one figure an added dimension of vitality is created by the inclusion of candles as a light source—a device learned from her earlier contact with the Utrecht Caravaggio School. *The Gay Cavaliers* (FIG. 36), signed with Leyster's monogram on the beer tankard, uses a single candle to show us the nocturnal revelry of two happily intoxicated young men. On the left, a boy, partially hidden by shadow, dressed in blue pants and a brown jacket, eagerly gulps the last drops from an uplifted jug which he holds with both hands, while on the right the shimmering candle-light reveals the dramatically gesticulating figure of his inebriated companion: a youth dressed in red who holds his lighted pipe aloft in one hand and appears not to mind the fact that he has drained his tankard to the last drop. Even the unattended candle seems to lurch to one side in this jovial scene of drunken abandonment.

Whereas *The Gay Cavaliers* is a "noisy" picture, other paintings, such as *The Rejected Offer* (FIG. 37), suggest a silent tableau—corresponding to the quiet aura that so frequently pervades Dutch interior scenes. *The Rejected Offer* is characteristic of the Dutch fascination for risqué subject matter in the guise of innocuous domesticity, for here, despite the apparent calmness of mood, we have a crass offer of money in exchange for certain intimate services. That the fur-capped intruder's proposition has been firmly rejected is understood through the eloquent silence of the woman who averts her head and continues her needlework. The displaying of such a picture in a Dutch home served not only to remind the beholder of the dangers of life but also as moral admonishment. The particular poetry that persists, despite the subject matter, was continued by the twentieth-century German artist Käthe Kollwitz in her scenes of domestic life in which she too used the device of a woman bent over her sewing illuminated by a single light source.

Leyster has left us a few signed and dated portraits which are good examples of the type of portraiture popular in Holland early in the seventeenth century when the prosperous middle class eagerly commissioned realistic images to hang in their homes. The sitters are portrayed half-length, wearing their black, Calvinist clothes, and their faces radiate good health and self-contentment. In Leyster's portraits of women the cheerful countenances are framed by tight-fitting caps and by the white millstone collar so in favor at the time. White lace cuffs adorn the austere black dresses, and occasionally a sitter is portrayed holding a book, presumably the Bible (FIG. 38).

At the end of the sixteenth century the University of Leiden laid out a Botanical Garden, and it was there that the first tulip was cultivated. Many

Dutch painters were understandably motivated to capture the beauty and structure of the new flower on their sketch pads, and Leyster became particularly well-known for her illustrations of tulips for a book published on that subject in 1643.

It was primarily as a genre painter that Leyster made her reputation, and an important study of her work points out that she was one of the first to paint intimate genre scenes in Holland.[1] It was customary at this time for artists to specialize in one type of painting; Hals was a portraitist, Claesz a still-life painter, Ruisdael a landscapist, and Vermeer a genre painter. It was the Golden Age of painting in The Netherlands, for the wealthy burghers were proud of their houses and took delight in hanging veristic reproductions of themselves, their daily lives, their possessions, and their country on the walls of their comfortable homes.

Because of their professional success, Judith and her husband were also able to enjoy the security of a home, and their last residence was a house purchased in Heemstede near Haarlem in 1648. There in the village of Heemstede she died in 1660, leaving behind her husband who survived her by eight years.

FIG. 34 JUDITH LEYSTER, *The Serenade*, 1629

FIG. 35 JUDITH LEYSTER, *The Flute Player*

FIG. 36 JUDITH LEYSTER, *The Gay Cavaliers*

FIG. 37 JUDITH LEYSTER, *The Rejected Offer*, 1631

FIG. 38 JUDITH LEYSTER, *Portrait of a Woman*, 1635

FIG. 39 ELISABETTA SIRANI, *Self-Portrait*

7

ELISABETTA SIRANI
1638·1665

I N BOLOGNA, which had boasted women artists in the two previous centuries,[1] the way was paved for a proliferation of women painters in the seventeenth century. One of the most extraordinary was Elisabetta Sirani, who, though she died mysteriously at the age of twenty-seven, managed in her short life to become a much sought-after professional artist and an instructor of a whole generation of women painters. Her teaching began with her two sisters, Anna Maria and Barbara, and soon extended to Ginevra Cantofoli, Vincenza Fabbri, Veronica Franchi, and Lucrezia Scarfaglia, all of whose religious paintings adorn the churches and monasteries of Bologna.[2]

Elisabetta, born on 8 January 1638, was the eldest daughter of the painter Giovanni Andrea Sirani, who had been a pupil of the leading Italian Baroque painter Guido Reni. Anna Maria, the next daughter, lived a normal life-span (1645–1715), and the third painter-daughter, Barbara, married a musician by the name of Borgognoni. The one son in the family, Antonio Maria, after studying philosophy and medicine, received his doctoral degree 24 September 1670.

Very early in life Elisabetta's talents were recognized, and she was given commissions by clergymen, senators, and noble families. Economic necessity also forced her into this professional role. Her father, incapacitated by gout, became a chronic invalid and could no longer support his family, so Elisabetta's productivity became indispensable to the household budget.

It was already the custom of painters at this time to keep a list of their completed works in order to be able to prove their authenticity should disputes arise. Elisabetta followed this practice, and fortunately her handwritten record containing a year-by-year enumeration of painted works, often with a short description and the name of the buyer, has been preserved. The list begins with commissions received at the age of seventeen, and 150 paintings are mentioned by Sirani, although her biographer, Count Malvasia,

81

who knew the family well, commented that the list did not represent her entire output, for he personally knew of other small works executed secretly (without her father's knowledge) to help her mother's finances.[3]

Elisabetta easily handled a wide range of subjects: religious, allegorical, mythological, as well as portraits. Although not especially innovative, she shows a great competence in her handling of figures and a penchant for elegant heads with large eyes, long noses, and small, rose-bud mouths.

Her studio became tantamount to a tourist attraction, and she was visited by many important dignitaries. Her account of the visit in 1664 to her studio of Cosimo, Crown Prince of Tuscany, does not conceal her pride at the fact that the prince came "to see my pictures. In his presence I worked on a painting of Prince Leopold, his uncle, in which the three specific virtues of this great house were referred to: 'Justice' assisted by 'Charity' and 'Prudence', all sketched out quite close to the child who is being suckled by 'Charity'. . . . Finally he [Cosimo] ordered a Blessed Virgin for himself, and I did it immediately, in time for him to have the picture dry before his return to Florence."[4]

Another pleasurable visit noted by Elisabetta was the occasion (1665) upon which "the Duchess of Brunswick was in our house to watch me paint. In her presence I executed a little cupid, one year in age, symbolizing true love."[5]

In addition to painting, Elisabetta wrote poetry, played the harp, and etched.[6] Most of the etchings, which are of religious subjects, date from her youthful years. Apparently, as she matured and established a reputation, her time was monopolized by commissions for paintings.

Suddenly, however, the promising career of the multi-talented Sirani came to an abrupt end in a death which is still shrouded in mystery. During the season of Lent in 1665 she felt and complained of stomach pains, but they passed. Then in August she felt them again and died abruptly on the 28th of the month. Her father, suspicious at the suddenness of her death, ordered a post-mortem examination. This took place the next day, and according to the doctors' report revealed no specific cause of death. Not satisfied by the report and convinced that an envious maid, who had recently been reprimanded by the family, had in fact poisoned his daughter, old Sirani took the case to court. Although the trial of the maid, Luca Tolomelli, produced a verdict of "not guilty," Count Malvasia, the family friend who recorded Elisabetta's career, was among those who were not convinced. Here is his view published just thirteen years after the event:

The poison then certainly, if it was poison, was foul and commonplace, like a caustic or burning lye, because after the body had been opened (so

82

those who saw it report, for I myself just did not have the heart to do so), the ventricle was found to be pierced with holes, even though the doctors, who first said so, finally changed their minds—with their fantasizing that it had not been a violent death, but a natural one; and if by poison, then it had arisen there spontaneously, and it was possible that it could generate itself inside a body, especially that of a woman, through the effects of feverfew, in this case a particularly vivacious and spirited woman, concealing to the highest degree her craving for a perhaps coveted husband, denied to her by her father.[7]

A Bolognese medical journal in 1898 took up the case and concluded that Elisabetta died of an ulcer in her stomach.[8] More recent opinion[9] tends to side with Count Malvasia since he was intimate with the Sirani family and had spoken with the doctors who examined the corpse.

The citizens of Bologna were shocked at the artist's sudden and premature death, and they gave her a funeral of gigantic proportions. As Malvasia wrote, "The city of Bologna has done her honor with a magnificent funeral as she did honor to Bologna." An announcement for the ceremony, specifying that an oration and poems would be delivered, refers to Elisabetta as "Most Famous Painter." The oration, entitled "The Lamented Paintbrush," was given by Giovanni Luigi Picinardi, distinguished Prior of the Lawyers at the University of Bologna. His lengthy tribute mentioned that many foreign patrons and distinguished persons had visited her studio, thereby gracing the city of Bologna. He eulogized her rare artistic talent and her estimable personal qualities.

The most spectacular feature of Elisabetta's funeral was the catafalque designed by one of the city artists to represent the Temple of Fame, which filled the nave of the church. Set high inside the towering structure of imitation marble was a life-size effigy of the artist shown seated at work before her easel (FIG. 44). Steps led up to the lifelike figure, and a small dome capped the tall octagonal structure. The choice of her grave site was the final honor accorded to her by her native city: she was buried next to Guido Reni.

Thus, an impressive city-wide service with especially commissioned sculpture, architecture, music, oratory, and poems marked the death of this seventeenth-century woman artist who today is scarcely known.

FIG. 40 ELISABETTA SIRANI, *Sibyl*

FIG. 41 Elisabetta Sirani, *Madonna of the Turtledove*

FIG. 42 Elisabetta Sirani, *Mary Magdalen*, 1660

FIG. 43 ELISABETTA SIRANI, *St. Anthony of Padua*

FIG. 44 Catafalque design for funeral of Elisabetta Sirani

FIG. 45 Netherlandish Master, *Portrait of Maria Sibylla Merian*, 1679

8 MARIA SIBYLLA MERIAN
1647·1717

W HAT A BOLD SPIRIT of adventure must have possessed this seventeenth-century scholar who, at the age of fifty-five, sailed across the Atlantic to live in the jungles of South America for two years! Maria Sibylla Merian's interest in natural history was so great that after several decades of writing and illustrating books on the insects and flowers of Europe, she felt compeled to expand her knowledge by recording the exotic wild life of Dutch Guiana.

Maria Sibylla was born into a family of engravers in Frankfurt am Main, Germany, in 1647. Her father, Matthaeus Merian the Elder, was an etcher and a book publisher who ran a large establishment and with whom aspiring print-makers like the famous Czech Wenceslaus Hollar came to study. The painter and writer Joachim Sandrart, who is best remembered today for his valuable biographies of Northern artists, worked in Merian's studio, which at that time was generally considered to be the center for printing and publishing in Germany.

Matthaeus died when Maria was four years old, and the same year her mother married Jacob Marrel, a German-born painter who was associated with the Utrecht circle of artists and specialized in flower paintings. It was he who recognized Maria's talents and encouraged her to become an artist by teaching her the rudiments of his craft and taking her with him on field trips. Another young pupil of Marrel's was Johann Andreas Graff, who is principally known to us today as the husband of Maria Sibylla Merian. Graff has left us an interesting drawing (dated 1658) showing the studio in which they all worked.[1] After studying with Marrel, Maria's future husband spent two years in Vienna and four years in Rome before returning to Frankfurt. The young painter-couple married in 1665, and their first daughter, Johanna, was born three years later. Shortly thereafter the small family moved to Graff's hometown, Nuremberg, where Maria began methodically to explore and paint the world of nature. She wrote, "From my youth I have been interested in insects. First I started with the silkworms in my native Frankfurt am Main. After that . . . I started to collect all the caterpillars I could find in order to observe their changes . . . and I painted them very carefully on parchment.''[2] By 1678, the year of the birth of her second daughter, Dorothea, she had embarked on her first ambitious work, a description of the insects of Europe. The book, *Der Raupen wunderbare Verwandelung und sonderbare Blumennahrung* (The Miraculous Transformation and Unusual Flower-Food of Caterpillars), was published the following year and was well received, partly because of the dazzling realism and microscopic clarity of the engravings.[3] The frontispiece is a colorful wreath of many different kinds of flowers interspersed with beetles, a bumblebee, and other insects. The next year the industrious painter-scholar brought out a book on flowers, entitled *Neues Blumenbuch* (A New Book of Flowers). In these publications Maria was helped technically by the contemporary switch from woodcut illustration to copper-plate engraving which enables more precise work with less manual effort.

At about this time her marriage began to flounder. Partly due to his difficult personality Graff encountered some personal and legal problems which forced him to leave the country for a period. Thus, when Maria's stepfather died in 1681, she took the occasion to leave her husband's domicile and return to her mother's home, taking the children with her. Back in Frankfurt she avidly continued her studies of plants and insects and in 1683 published a second volume on European insects.[4]

Perhaps partially as a result of her broken marriage, Maria now became deeply involved with a popular new religious sect, the Labadists, who did not believe in formal marriage ties. This sect had been founded as an evangelistic cult by a French mystic, Jean de Labadie, who renounced the doctrines of the Roman Catholic Church. Though he had died in 1674, his followers maintained a fervid colony that centered in a castle in the northern Dutch province of Friesland. Caspar Merian, an older half-brother of Maria, had already entered this retreat. Anna Maria van Schurman, Dutch artist, poet, and multi-linguist, was another of the devotées of the cult. At last, unable to resist any longer the attractions which the quietist refuge of the Labadists seemed to offer, Maria, with her daughters, made the long trip from Frankfurt to Friesland and joined the group in the castle in 1685. Graff visited her the following year, but he could not persuade his wife to leave. In fact, she desisted from any further use of his name and even made a will calling herself a widow though Graff lived until 1701.

The proximity of the retreat to the town of Bosch and the city of Leeuwarden made it possible for Maria to examine in detail the cabinet collections of insects owned by prominent Frieslanders, many of whom were Labadists. She also used this opportunity to learn the Dutch language and then went onto Amsterdam to see the museums and, especially, to study the collections from the East and West Indies. She wrote that she found the private collection of the director of the East India Company singularly instructive. As for the West Indies, she was so enchanted with their animal specimens that she began to explore the possibility of traveling there to see the native species for herself. She was particularly concerned about the difficulty of preserving caterpillars and other larvae, and she thought she might be able to compensate for the paucity of specimens by making colored drawings of living examples on the spot. Her driving impulse was to determine the nature of the foreign insects' metamorphosis and their choice of food.

The evangelistic Labadists had established several missions, and luckily one was in the Dutch possession of Surinam in South America. So Maria and her younger daughter Dorothea, also an artist, were able to set sail for the colony in 1699. They found that the capital city, Paramaribo, consisted of 500 houses made of wood and two of brick, and that, although most of the jungle was uninhabitable, the colonists were thriving on cocoa and sugar-cane production. In her writing Maria, admiring the American cherry, chided these profit-seekers for neglecting the cultivation of more native fruits.

The two Merians were able to visit a Labadist plantation, near the jungle, and there they began collecting and studying caterpillars. Later, when they became more courageous, they journeyed down the Commewijne River, despite the fact that Maria had contracted yellow fever. The ever-inquiring artist had expanded the scope of her work and was also painting the exotic birds and flora. In these watercolors we see that scientific curiosity is well blended with aesthetic considerations, for in addition to an exacting veri-similitude, the subjects of the artist's attention are elegantly placed in relation to each other and in obedience to laws of formal composition. Maria shows a fondness for curves in her designs, and in the striking depiction of an egret entwined by a snake, she even thinks to include the shadow cast by the snake on the body of the bird (FIG. 48).

She was fascinated with the ants and wrote, "There are very large ants in America who strip trees bare as brooms in one night; they have two curved teeth, built like scissors, and with these they cut the leaves from the trees and let them fall down, so that the tree looks like a European tree during winter-time."[5]

One of her most startling paintings shows the hunting spider attacking a hummingbird which has just been dragged from her nest of eggs (FIG. 49). Maria's own account states:

> I found many large dark colored spiders on the guava tree which take up their abode in the large cocoon of a caterpillar; for they do not spin webs, as some travelers have tried to make us believe. Their bodies are entirely covered with hair, and they are armed with long pointed teeth, with which they bite severely and inflict dangerous wounds by injecting some kind of liquid. Their common food is ants, which they capture with ease as they run upon the trees; for, like all other spiders, they are furnished with eight eyes, two placed above and two below, two on the right side, and a like number on the left. When they cannot obtain ants, they carry off even small birds from their nests, and suck the blood from their bodies. . . . These spiders seize upon hummingbirds when sitting on their nests. This bird was formerly used by the priests of Surinam as an article of food, and I am assured that they were prohibited from eating any other kind of food.[6]

The deterioration of her health from the bout with yellow fever forced Maria to return after almost two years in the tropics to Amsterdam where she arrived in September 1701 and took up residence with her married daughter Johanna and her husband. Maria now had her own cabinet of specimens and copious notes which she was urged to publish. The result was her magnum opus, *Metamorphosis Insectorum Surinamensium* (The Metamorphosis of Surinam Insects), published in Amsterdam in 1705 in both Latin and Dutch and containing sixty plates engraved from her watercolors. By now Maria through self-education had achieved a name for herself as a scientist, and her artistic ability simply served as a tool to accomplish her scholarly research.[7]

Maria next turned her attention to completing the third and final volume of her European insect book which was published along with a second edition of the first two volumes. Scholarly work has never been known as a munificent source of income, and Merian's books were no exception. In a new will, which she drew up at this point, she stated that she was penniless and supported by her children.

Maria's zeal for entomology was contagious and rapidly spread to her elder daughter Johanna and her husband, and in 1714 the couple left for Surinam to do more collecting. Soon after their departure Maria suffered a stroke and presumably went to live with her other daughter Dorothea and her husband, George Gsell, a painter and engraver who made a portrait of his mother-in-law in 1714. Maria did not live to see the return of her older daughter from Dutch Guiana but died at the age of seventy in Amsterdam on 13 January 1717. The death certificate was signed by a Registrar of the Poor—an ironic final witness to the long career of this distinguished artist-scientist whose works were to aid the nature studies of no less a kindred spirit than Goethe. A fitting tribute has been paid to Merian by the natural scientists who have named insects and plants after this extraordinary, pioneering woman of the seventeenth century.[8]

FIG. 46 MARIA SIBYLLA MERIAN, *Watercolor from Surinam Notebook*

FIG. 47 MARIA SIBYLLA MERIAN, *Watercolor from Surinam Notebook*

FIG. 48 MARIA SIBYLLA MERIAN, *Watercolor from Surinam Notebook*

FIG. 49 MARIA SIBYLLA MERIAN, Plate XVIII, *Metamorphosis Insectorum Surinamensium*

FIG. 50 MARIA SIBYLLA MERIAN, *Watercolor from Surinam Notebook*

FIG. 51 CONSTANTIN NETSCHER, *Rachel Ruysch in her Studio*

9 RACHEL RUYSCH
1664·1750

T HE NAME OF RACHEL RUYSCH has never suffered obscurity; she has always been recognized as one of the greatest still-life painters ever produced by Holland. Her speciality was flower painting—a subject which came into its own during the Baroque period when other new categories were also being introduced into art, such as landscapes and genre scenes.

It would be a mistake to presume that this new category of painting was somehow "women's work." Many male artists earned their living as flower painters in the seventeenth century: de Heem in Holland, Jan Brueghel in Flanders, Arellano in Spain, Baschenis and Porpora in Italy. In her youth Ruysch studied with a successful local practitioner of the art, Willem van Aelst, but she soon went on to make popular her own very distinctive style. It is a style that unmistakably differentiates her work from that of the other flower painters, for an element of life and sometimes menacing surprise inhabits her floral arrangements. We have only to look at her still life from the Ashmolean Museum (FIG. 52) in which a coiled snake is ferociously poised with an open mouth ready to snap up a grasshopper, while two snails slither past and a field mouse watches quietly from the underbrush. In her Glasgow still life (FIG. 53) depicting a great variety of flowers against a tree trunk one sees in the foreground a lizard catching a butterfly in its mouth. Ruysch often differs too from her most famous male colleagues in the North by varying the settings for her flowers, abandoning the formula of a vase of flowers on a table to place her horticultural studies in a woodland or forest environment.[1] Her deep, vivid colors add a sparkling quality to the drama of her insect-and-animal inhabited still life.

Rachel was born into an educated Amsterdam family in 1664. Her father was a professor of Anatomy and Botany, as well as being an amateur painter, and her mother was the daughter of the architect Pieter Post. Her sister, Anna Elisabeth, also became a still-life painter, and both women managed to combine marriage and work. At the age of twenty-nine, in 1693, Rachel married Juriaen Pool, a portraitist in Amsterdam. She gave birth to ten children but never broke off her activities as an artist, always signing her works with her maiden name.

Industrious and ambitious, Ruysch and Pool moved to The Hague hoping to better their fortunes in the Dutch capital. They both became members of the artist's guild there in 1701. Their reputation began to spread abroad, and seven years later the Elector Palatine invited the couple to be his court painters in Düsseldorf. The comfort and patronage of German court life apparently suited the two artists, and in time they became intimate enough with the Elector Johann Wilhelm to have him act as godfather to one of their sons. In 1716 upon the death of the German ruler, they returned to Amsterdam. During Ruysch's eight years at the distinguished court on the Rhine all of her paintings were kept in the Elector's collection except for a few which he sent as gifts to the Grand Duke of Tuscany. Of these works now in the Galleria Pitti, Florence, is here illustrated one of fruit and vegetables in which a nest of eggs in the foreground has just been raided by a lizard who is busy scooping out the contents of a stolen egg (FIG. 54).

Usually Ruysch signed her paintings with an ornate signature, but in a still life (FIG. 55) instead of her autograph she showed herself mirrored in a glass vase. Close scrutiny reveals that she included not only a reflection of herself painting but also the window of her studio. In her still life in Raleigh (FIG. 56) the artist has repeatedly caught her own image on the open lid of a watch. The device of incorporating one's own reflection onto a shiny surface goes back to at least Jan van Eyck, the fifteenth-century Flemish artist, who included his own image in the *Madonna and Child of the Canon van der Paele* where the artist's features can be seen in the polished armor of St. George. Clara Peeters, a Flemish still-life painter of the seventeenth century, recorded her own reflection several times on a pewter pitcher in a work now in the Prado Museum, and her self-portrait with brushes and palette is mirrored four times on the silver goblet in a still life at the Karlsruhe Museum.

A veritable proliferation of women artists took place all over Europe in the seventeenth century. While Ruysch was composing her clusters of flowers and fruit and Peeters her vessels and dishes of food, Catharina Ykens of Antwerp was combining garlands of flowers with religious scenes. In France Louise Moillon executed still lifes with a complementing human figure, for example, *The Fruit Vendor* (Wildenstein Gallery, New York), and the Boulogne sisters were painting trophies of war for the palace at Versailles and other such vanities of earthly life, a type of painting called *Vanitas*. In Italy Elena Recco and Margharita Caffi became noted flower painters, whereas in England Mary Beale, daughter of a pastor, created remarkable portraits, and in Spain Luisa Roldán was appointed Sculptor of the Royal Court of Charles II.

The grand and bombastic portrait of Rachel Ruysch done by her compatriot Constantin Netscher (FIG. 51) gives us some hint of the high esteem in which she was held. Around her neck on a blue ribbon hangs the medal presented to her by the Elector Palatine, and overhead a cupid is about to crown her while the winged figure of "Fame" ascends to heaven carrying the artist's palette and brushes and heralding her arrival with trumpet blasts. Meanwhile, back on earth, the artist regally points to one of her still lifes on the easel in a setting crowded with allusions to the arts while behind it all stands the goddess Minerva, patron of the arts.

But such allegorical support was not necessary. Ruysch was in fact widely acclaimed, and her paintings brought prices that ranged from 750 to 1250 guilders, comparing favorably with those received by her Dutch predecessor, Rembrandt, who rarely was given more than 500 guilders for a work.[2] She also influenced the work of other Dutch painters: Anna Elisabeth Ruysch, Elias van der Broek, and the noted Jan van Huysum, and lived to the vintage age of eighty-six, painting right up until her death in 1750.

FIG. 52 RACHEL RUYSCH, *Still Life*

FIG. 53 RACHEL RUYSCH, *Still Life*

FIG. 54 RACHEL RUYSCH, *Fruit, Flowers, and Insects*, 1716

FIG. 55 RACHEL RUYSCH, *Flowers*　　　　　　FIG. 56 RACHEL RUYSCH, *A Vase of Flowers*

FIG. 57 ROSALBA CARRIERA, *Self-Portrait Holding Portrait of her Sister*, 1715

10 ROSALBA CARRIERA
1675·1757

"PROLIFIC" AND "LONG-LIVED" are two adjectives which appropriately describe the Venetian painter Rosalba Carriera. It is difficult to pick up the catalog of any major museum and not find one of her works listed. The Dresden Museum alone counts 157 pastels and seventeen miniatures by her. The small size of her pictures and the assistance she received from a sister enabled her to keep up with the steady procession of clients who visited her studio. The popularity of her work resulted in invitations to Paris, Modena, and Vienna and in commissions to paint such monarchs as Louis XV of France and Augustus III of Poland.

Art historians credit her with introducing the pastel portrait into France and with making it the vogue in Paris.[1] Carriera paved the way for Quentin de La Tour and Jean Etienne Liotard to pursue successful careers fulfiling the insatiable demand for portraits in the delicate new medium after her whirlwind conquest of Paris in 1720–1721.

Despite her successes abroad Carriera seems to have been deeply attached to her native Venice and could never be persuaded to stay away very long. The family house, known today as the "Casa Biondetti," because of its nineteenth-century owners, is on the Grand Canal just next to the Palazzo da Mula, made famous by the Impressionist artist Monet who painted it several times. Rosa Alba, as she was christened but whose first two names became combined, and her two younger sisters Angela and Giovanna received instruction in music, French, and Latin. Their grandfather had been a painter, and from her earliest years Rosalba exhibited a strong artistic bent. As a public official her father earned only a modest salary, augmented by his wife's earnings as a lace-maker. Before long the eldest daughter was drawing patterns for her mother's lace, but soon she turned to the more lucrative work of decorating snuff boxes. She entered the studio of Giuseppe Diamantini and later that of Antonio Balestra to learn anatomy, and then she in turn gave lessons to her two sisters.

In her early twenties, after having begun to produce miniatures, she was introduced to pastels through the Venetian artist, Gian Antonio Lazzari, who specialized in making pastel copies of oil paintings. Her interest in the medium's capacity for subtle nuance and speed of execution was quickened around 1700 when an old family friend Canon Ramelli sent her a large and splendid assortment of the colorful chalk bars from Rome. She became such a master of the medium and so successful with her portraits in pastel that by 1705 she was proposed for membership in the Academy of St. Luke in Rome and was unanimously elected. Academies were established in the sixteenth century in an effort to elevate the position of the artist and to distinguish him from a craftsman. Instruction was offered and a diploma granted on completion of studies. Honorary memberships were often bestowed by academies on people of exceptional talent, thus it was a sign of recognition accorded Carriera when the oldest of painting academies, St. Luke's in Rome, granted her membership. The academies in Bologna and Florence followed suit, and the Grand Duke Cosimo de' Medici III requested that she send a self-portrait for his collection in Florence. She responded with a pastel *Self-Portrait* of 1715 in which she shows herself holding a sketch of her sister Giovanna (FIG. 57).

Between 1712 and 1717 the Prince of Saxony made three trips to Venice and on each occasion he spent considerable time at Carriera's studio sitting for portraits of himself in various poses as well as purchasing pastels and miniatures for the collection of his father, Augustus II, in Dresden. In one of the most impressive oil portraits of him by Carriera (FIG. 58) he can be seen bewigged and wearing a resplendent red coat. He later succeeded to his father's expanded domain with the title of "Augustus III, King of Poland." He was unsuccessful, however, in persuading his favorite portraitist to join his far-off court.

Other royal visitors who came to Carriera's studio for portrait sittings were Maximilian II of Bavaria, Charles VI, Elector Palatine, and Frederick IV, King of Norway and Denmark who ordered in addition to his own portrait those of twelve Venetian ladies to take back to his Nordic court.

Among the French tourists was the financier and art collector Pierre Crozat, who insisted that the skilled pastellist visit him in Paris, an invitation which Carriera saw fit to accept only after the death of her father in 1719. By this time her sister Angela was married to the painter Giovanni Antonio Pellegrini, who had recently returned from England where he had contracted with the economist John Law to begin work soon on the ceiling of the Royal Bank in Paris. Therefore, it was a sizable party of Rosalba, Giovanna, their elderly mother, and the Pellegrinis who set off for Paris by carriage in March

1720. As Crozat promised, a spacious apartment with studio in his palace on Rue de Richelieu was made available to Rosalba for the duration of her visit, and the Pellegrinis were accommodated in a nearby inn.

A diary kept by Carriera from 5 April 1720 to 11 March 1721 gives us a reliable if disappointing sketchy outline of her year in Paris. Her mornings were dedicated to painting and her afternoons commited to sightseeing and social engagements. She saw the major works in all the galleries in Paris, including Rubens's series of paintings commissioned by Marie de' Medici for the Luxembourg Palace and of course journeyed out to see the Palace at Versailles.

In Paris Carriera started at the top: one of her first sitters was Louis XV who though a boy of ten was already King of France. After completing the portrait, Carriera was asked for copies by various members of the court and nobility, so that today more than one version of her portrait of the young king exists (FIG. 59). Needless to say, this impressive royal commission whetted the appetites of French artistocracy for pastels by Carriera, and her sister Giovanna helped her meet the flood of demands by filling in the draperies and the backgrounds of the portraits. The actual reins of government at this time were in the hands of the Regent Philip II, Duke of Orleans, who also honored the artist by visiting her studio.

The culmination of her artistic recognition came within six months of her arrival when the French Academy of Painting and Sculpture voted unanimously to elect her as a member—a distinction rarely conferred upon women this early in the history of the Academy. The usual trial period and presentation piece were waived in this case, and she was admited on the strength of her portrait of the King; only after her return to Venice did she send her diploma painting, a Muse holding a laurel wreath, which today is in the Louvre.

On the evening of 30 September 1720 Crozat decided the time had come to stun his fellow Parisians with yet another side of his multi-talented Venetian guest. He organized a concert to which the Regent and other French dignitaries were invited including the painter Antoine Watteau who has immortalized the evening by a sketch preserved in the Louvre.[2] The feature performer of the evening was Rosalba, a most accomplished violinist. She was joined by the late player Antoine Rebel, François Rebel, future director of the opera, Pacini of the Royal Choir, and as singers Giovanna Carriera, Madame de Lafosse, and Mlle d'Argenon. The following February Rosalba, according to her diary, began a portrait of Watteau, perhaps the last portrayal of him since he died six months later.

However, in March of 1721 social and professional success could not keep the homesick Venetian in Paris indefinitely. The Carrieras began a return trip which was to consume two months. An outbreak of the plague unexpectedly closed the city of Marseilles to travelers, and a lengthy detour through Strasbourg and the Tyrol was forced on the family.

Carriera's reputation had not waned in Italy during her absence. The Duke of Modena, Renaldo d'Este, who had three marriageable daughters through whom he hoped to arrange political alliances, had already been advised by his ambassador in Paris to engage Rosalba Carriera to make portraits of his daughters which could then be sent to ducal mothers. Consequently in 1723 Rosalba and Giovanna traveled to Modena to paint the young ladies. The plan worked almost too well, especially for Enrichetta, the prettiest of the three, who received several conflicting offers of marriage.

The next courtly invitation was an imperial one. In 1730 Charles VI, ruler of the Holy Roman Empire, asked the artist to visit Vienna. Continuing to work in a Rococo style Carriera did his portrait and that of the Empress as well as other members of the nobility. Her Austrian stay lasted half a year, and the letters of Rosalba and Giovanna to their mother describe numerous excursions to parks, palaces, and convents. This was the last trip the sisters were to make together, for Giovanna died of tuberculosis in 1737. The bereaved older sister sank into a melancholy which prevented her from working. Gradually her interest was renewed as she found from among her own students some talented and willing apprentices to assist her with the unabating number of portrait commissions.

Then without warning at the age of seventy-one she became blind. Her last work was done in 1746 for her old patron, Augustus III. She hesitated three years before submiting to a risky operation for cataracts, and afterward she was able to see, but only dimly, for a brief time. Although she courageously underwent a further operation, it was unsuccessful, and she remained totally blind for the last seven years of her life. Angela Pellegrini after her husband's death had returned home and was on hand to read aloud to her sister. Then in her eighty-second year Rosalba quietly died, leaving as the result of her enormous output a large fortune which passed on to Angela along with the gifts which she had received, such as a Watteau painting, a medal struck in her honor by the Holy Roman Emperor, Meissen porcelain from Augustus III, and her violin.

FIG. 58 ROSALBA CARRIERA, *Augustus III, King of Poland*

FIG. 59 ROSALBA CARRIERA, *Louis XV as a Boy*

FIG. 60 ROSALBA CARRIERA, *Allegory of Painting*

FIG. 61 ROSALBA CARRIERA, *Miniature of Venus and Child*

FIG. 62 ROSALBA CARRIERA, *Cardinal Polignac*

FIG. 63 ANGELICA KAUFFMANN, *Angelica Hesitating Between the Arts of Music and Painting*

11 ANGELICA KAUFFMANN
1741·1807

As a painter of note, Angelica Kauffmann's image today adorns the Austrian 100-schilling bank note. That country's right to claim the Swiss-born artist as its own was established during her lifetime when, coming of legal age, Kauffmann declared allegiance to Emperor Josef II of Austria.[1] Nevertheless her prolonged residences in England and Italy made her a citizen of Europe.

Angelica's father was an itinerant painter from the Tyrol, and while in the Swiss town of Chur his one child Maria Anna Angelica Catherina was born in 1741. Her youth was spent traveling from town to town in northern Italy while her father fulfilled various sporadic commissions. The high-spirited little girl first trained to become a musician, singing and learning to play several stringed instruments. She was also adept at drawing and fascinated by her father's profession. In Milan, where they settled for three years, she was able to study the Renaissance and Baroque holdings of private galleries, and, when her mother died, the sixteen-year-old artist had a chance to try her hand helping her father to decorate the parish church of his native Tyrolian village of Schwarzenberg near Bregenz. This experience only heightened her interest in becoming an artist and forced upon her the most difficult decision of her life. Equally and enormously talented in both music and art, she knew by the age of nineteen that a total commitment had to be made to one or the other. She commemorated this dilemma in a self-portrait titled: *Angelica Hesitating Between the Arts of Music and Painting* (FIG. 63). Angelica seems to have made her choice in this picture: with her left hand she points to "Art," while clasping the hand of "Music" with her right in a sad gesture of farewell.

Once the decision was made, father and daughter embarked on an itinerary of Italian cities famous for their art collections. In the Uffizi Gallery in Florence she was given a private room in which to paint and to further her studies by copying the old masters. Here she met another visitor to the city,

117

the American painter Benjamin West, through whom she acquired numerous English patrons. Traveling farther south to Rome and Naples, she became acquainted with Nathaniel Dance, the English painter, who fell deeply in love with her—a fact alluded to by Boswell in his chatty *On the Grand Tour*. Among her portraits at this time is that of the great actor David Garrick (FIG. 64), in whose traveling company Dance's brother was a performer. During the sitting Garrick composed the following poem to the artist:

> While thus you paint with ease and grace,
> And spirit all your own,
> Take, if you please, my mind and face,
> But let my heart alone.

She was also introduced to the noted German archaeologist and classical scholar, Johann Joachim Winckelmann, whose portrait she painted in Rome in 1764. As Winckelmann wrote, Angelica was a rare person, proficient in German, Italian, English, and French and a beauty and musician as well. A vivacious, extroverted being who made friends easily, her company was much sought after. Goethe wrote in his diary, "She is a tireless worker, both at painting and at studying, and I greatly enjoy looking at works of art with her."[2]

When she was twenty-four, the Academy of St. Luke in Rome elected her to its membership, and the following year her work was so celebrated that she was invited by Lady Wentworth, the wife of the former English ambassador to Venice, to accompany her party to London. Within six months of her arrival Kauffmann was likened to Van Dyck and Rubens. Lords and ladies, as well as the Royal Family, vied for her neo-classical paintings. In a year's time she had earned enough money to purchase her own home in Golden Square and to invite her father to join her in London.

Her English friends made certain that upon arrival in London she was introduced to Sir Joshua Reynolds who soon became her close friend. They quickly reciprocated with portraits of each other (FIG. 65) and spent considerable time together. In 1768 Reynolds and Kauffmann were among the thirty-six founding members of the British Royal Academy. In fact, Mary Moser and Kauffmann were the only two women admitted into this august body. Johann Zoffany did a painting of his colleagues entitled *The Academicians of the Royal Academy* in which the thirty-four male members are all portrayed in person in a classroom but the female founders are merely represented by bust portraits hanging on the wall.

When a special exhibition was arranged for the visiting King of Denmark in 1768, Kauffmann contributed four history paintings. These works were shown again at the first exhibition of the Royal Academy where she and West—both actually foreigners—were ranked together as the two leading painters of classical history then in London. Examples of Kauffmann's history paintings are *The Sadness of Telemachus* (FIG. 66, Metropolitan Museum) and *Pliny the Younger and his Mother at Misenum, 19 A.D.* (Princeton University Art Museum).

Among foreign noblemen visiting her studio at this time was a young Swede who identified himself as the Count de Horn. He was persuasive as well as handsome, and when he proposed marriage to the painter, she found herself accepting his offer. Later, to her utter dismay, she discovered that her new husband was not only already married, but a commoner named Brandt. The whole truth of this ingeniously perpetrated hoax was revealed when the real Count de Horn arrived in London and, upon being received by the Queen, was congratulated on his marriage to Kauffmann—a bit of information which flabbergasted the count. Brandt's brashness was not deterred. He first tried forcibly to abduct Angelica, and failing that he then demanded money from her father. Before he stopped pestering the family, he had wrested several hundred pounds from the embarrassed Kauffmanns. Still there was no freedom for Angelica. Because she was a Catholic, she could not re-marry until Brandt's death which conveniently occured in 1780. Immediately, and at almost forty years of age, she married a man fifteen years her senior, the Italian decorative artist Antonio Zucchi, who had been occupied many years painting scenes for houses designed by the English neo-classical architect Robert Adam. Although both painters were engaged in successful careers, Angelica's father was ill, and doctors suspected that he could not recuperate in the English climate. The newly married couple decided to return to the Continent, taking the elderly father with them. He survived long enough to visit his native town again but died in Venice. The couple continued to Rome where they took a house on the Via Sistina near the Spanish Steps. Commissions for Angelica flowed in from a variety of impressive customers: Empress Catherine II of Russia, Emperor Josef II of Austria, King Stanislas II of Poland, the King and Queen of Sardinia, and Sir William Hamilton, at that time British Ambassador to the Kingdom of the Two Sicilies. After painting a large portrait of the family of King Ferdinand IV and Queen Maria Carolina of Naples (FIG. 67), Kauffmann was offered the position of court artist which she refused, preferring to remain in Rome. Zucchi meanwhile busied himself taking care of the practical matters of obtaining canvas and frames for his illustrious wife and arranging the transportation of her completed works. Goethe (FIG. 68), whose two Italian trips acquainted him with the Rome of 1786–1788, described his frequent encounters with Kauffmann as follows:

> I dined with Angelica—it has become a tradition that I am her guest every Sunday. In the morning we had driven to the Barberini palace to see the Leonardo da Vinci and Raphael's portrait of his mistress. It is a great pleasure to look at paintings with Angelica, for she has a trained eye and knows a great deal about the technical side of painting. Moreover, she is sensitive to all that is true and beautiful, and incredibly modest.[3]

> Last Sunday I went with Angelica to see Prince Aldobrandini's pictures, particularly an admirable Leonardo da Vinci. Considering her great talent and her fortune, she is not as happy as she deserves to be. She is tired of commissions, but her old husband thinks it wonderful that so much money should roll in for what is often easy work. She would like to paint to please herself and have more leisure to study and take pains, and she could easily do this. They have no children and they cannot even spend the interest on her capital: indeed, they could live on the money she earns every day by working moderately hard. But she doesn't do anything about it and she won't. She talks to me very frankly; I have told her my opinion, given her advice and I try to cheer her up whenever we meet. What's the use of talking about misery and misfortune when people who have enough of everything do not know how to use it or enjoy it? For a woman, she has extraordinary talent.[4]

Angelica lived on for twelve years after her husband's death, and perhaps she found some of the happiness Goethe felt she deserved in the continued admiration and demand for her works. When she died at the age of sixty-six in 1807, her will generously provided for the servants who had been attending her, and her paintings and books went to her cousin Johann Kauffmann. Antonio Canova, Rome's most revered sculptor and a personal friend of Angelica, arranged a funeral for the painter unparalleled in Rome since the death of Raphael. A letter describing Angelica's funeral to her cousins, the Bonomis, which was read into the minutes of the Royal Academy in London, reported that the church of S. Andrea delle Fratte was decorated as fit for nobility and that the funeral procession was one of the longest ever witnessed by Romans. Fifty Capuchin monks and fifty priests accompanied the bier through the city. The four tassels of the coffin were held by the first four *signori* of the Academy, followed by the rest of the academicians who held aloft two of her paintings for the crowds to see. In the church the paintings were placed on either side of the altar while nearby stood a bust of the artist in marble, finished just one month before her death by Canova.

Kauffmann had chosen to be buried in S. Andrea delle Fratte in order to have her tomb next to her husband's, whereas actually her position as an important painter warranted a place in the Pantheon along with Raphael and other distinguished artists. Therefore, on the first anniversary of her death in November 1808 the members of the Academy of St. Luke paid their colleague a final tribute by conducting a memorial service in the Pantheon at which they unveiled a new marble bust of the immortal Angelica Kauff-mann sculpted by her cousin Johann.

The characteristics of Kauffmann's style which differentiate her work from that of other neo-classical artists are the painterly, rather than linear contours of her figures and a pronounced vertical emphasis in composition—a tectonic building up of elements, even to the point of an occasional crowding of objects. Most noticeably she differs from her contemporaries by showing a negligible interest in virtuoso architectural detail or the inclusion of archaeo-logical memorabilia. She possessed a special talent for portraiture as seen in the refreshing informality of her portrait of the actor *David Garrick*. In her *Portrait of Sir Joshua Reynolds* of 1767 she combines an impression of the sitter's intellectual acuity with a relaxed friendly pose—in contrast to his own later self-portrait which is marked by a haughty stance, although it bears in common with the portrait by Kauffmann an accompanying bust of the mutually-revered Michelangelo. Kauffmann seems to have had the ability to put her sitters at ease, and this is observable even in the large formal group portraits of royalty and other dignitaries.

FIG. 64 ANGELICA KAUFFMANN, *Portrait of David Garrick*

FIG. 65   ANGELICA KAUFFMANN, *Portrait of Sir Joshua Reynolds*, 1767

FIG. 66 ANGELICA KAUFFMANN, *The Sadness of Telemachus*

FIG. 67 ANGELICA KAUFFMANN, *The Family of King Ferdinand IV and Queen Maria Carolina*, 1784

FIG. 68 ANGELICA KAUFFMAN, *Portrait of Goethe*

FIG. 69 ELISABETH VIGÉE-LEBRUN, *Self-Portrait*

12 ELISABETH VIGÉE LEBRUN
1755·1842

As PORTRAITIST to Queen Marie Antoinette Madame Marie Louise Elisabeth Vigée-Lebrun had earned a reputation which opened royal doors of patronage in all the capitals of Europe when the French Revolution forced her into twelve years of exile from her native land. Vigée-Lebrun, with her young daughter, escaped across the border into Italy where she was extremely well-received, especially as she made her way southward down the peninsula. In Naples she painted such prominent people as Queen Maria Carolina and Lady Emma Hamilton, whose name was soon to be linked with that of Admiral Nelson. Vienna, ruled by the Hapsburg relatives of Marie Antoinette, offered warm hospitality to the artist, thus encouraging her to stay for two and a half years, but it was in St. Petersburg that she remained longest. The Empress Catherine II received her with immediate enthusiasm, and, when Vigée-Lebrun was finally able to return to France six years later, she fondly referred to Russia as her second motherland.

Elisabeth was born in Paris in 1755. Her father was a pastel portrait painter who, quickly appreciating the early evidence of his daughter's talent, sent her to his colleague, the painter Davesne, to learn how to mix oil colors. When her father died prematurely, Vigée-Lebrun—still barely a child herself —set to work painting oil portraits in earnest to help pay for her younger brother's schooling. One of the earliest clients of this young prodigy was Count Shuvaloff, chamberlain of the Empress of Russia, whose portrait can be seen today in the North Carolina Museum of Art (FIG. 70).

In 1779 at the age of twenty-four Elisabeth began painting portraits of Marie Antoinette. Nine years earlier the French Queen had been given by her mother, Empress Maria Theresa of Austria, to King Louis XVI in a political marriage. Marie Antoinette was only a year older than her painter, and an easy rapport developed between the two women. In her *Memoires*, a long and informative journal conscientiously maintained through the year

1835, Vigée-Lebrun writes,

> I was so fortunate as to be on very pleasant terms with the Queen. When she heard that I had something of a voice we rarely had a sitting without singing some duets by Grétry together, for she was exceedingly fond of music. . . .
>
> One day I happened to miss the appointment she had given me for a sitting; I had suddenly become unwell. The next day I hastened to Versailles to offer my excuses. The Queen was not expecting me; she had had her horses harnessed to go out driving, and her carriage was the first thing I saw on entering the palace yard. I nevertheless went upstairs to speak with the chamberlains on duty. One of them, M. Campan, received me with a stiff and haughty manner, and bellowed at me in his stentorian voice, 'It was yesterday, madame, that Her Majesty expected you, and I am sure she is going out driving, and I am very sure she will give you no sitting today!' Upon my reply that I had simply come to take her Majesty's orders for another day, he went to the Queen, who at once had me conducted to her room. She was finishing her toilet, and was holding a book in her hand, hearing her daughter repeat a lesson. My heart was beating violently, for I knew that I was in the wrong. But the Queen looked up at me and said most amiably, 'I was waiting for you all the morning yesterday; what happened to you?'
>
> 'I am sorry to say, Your Majesty,' I replied, 'I was so ill that I was unable to comply with Your Majesty's commands. I am here to receive more now, and then I will immediately retire.'
>
> 'No, no! Do not go!' exclaimed the Queen. 'I do not want you to have made your journey for nothing!' She revoked the order for her carriage and gave me a sitting. I remember that, in my confusion and my eagerness to make a fitting response to her kind words, I opened my paint-box so excitedly that I spilled my brushes on the floor. I stooped down to pick them up. 'Never mind, never mind,' said the Queen, and, for aught I could say, she insisted on gathering them all up herself.[1]

When Vigée-Lebrun was proposed for membership in the Royal Academy of Painting, the nomination ran into difficulty because Jean-Baptiste Pierre, First Painter to the King, opposed the admission of any more women artists. Anne Vallayer-Coster and two other women were already members, and Pierre, unnecessarily fearful of a minority takeover, fumed that even three were too many. However, the monarchal interest shown by Marie Antoinette in Vigée-Lebrun's admission dissipated any such resistance, and in 1793 she was accepted into the venerable organization with her painting *Peace Bringing*

128

Abundance. Previously she had been elected into the Roman Academy of St. Luke, and subsequently, wherever she traveled, she received this professional recognition: the academies of Bologna, Florence, St. Petersburg, and Berlin all named her to membership.

In her private life Vigée-Lebrun's choice of a husband was a near disaster and is curiously reminiscent of Angelica Kauffmann's unfortunate experience in marriage. At the age of twenty she accepted the proposal of a Parisian art dealer named Jean-Baptiste Pierre Lebrun, but what promised to be a good professional match turned out to be a draining burden, for Lebrun was a chronic gambler who helped himself to a good part of his wife's earnings. They had only one child, a daughter, who was later to give her mother endless worries as a spoiled, willful girl in Russia. Domestic disappointments and responsibilities did not obstruct Vigée-Lebrun's sociable nature, however, and she became as famous for her musical soirées as for her paintings. Her *Memoires* note with satisfaction that sometimes her parties became so crowded that marshalls of France were to be seen sitting on the floor for want of chairs, and she boasted that the music performed in her home was the best to be heard in Paris. Her elegantly austere painting of *Angelica Catalini* (FIG. 74) commemorates one of these evenings when this young soprano recently arrived from Italy entertained by singing arias. The individuality of this work reflects the fact that it was not a commission; Vigée-Lebrun did the painting to hang in her own house as a pendant to her portrait of a contralto who also performed for her.

Despite competition among the first ladies of Paris in regard to whose weekly salon was judged the most distinguished, Vigée-Lebrun was on good terms with at least one retired rival. This was the former mistress of Louis XV, Mme du Barry, who invited the artist to stay with her in Louveciennes and to paint her portrait in several different poses. Vigée-Lebrun commented as follows on the Parisian society which she knew and enjoyed: "The women reigned then; the Revolution dethroned them."[2]

Although the events of 1789 temporarily left Vigée-Lebrun without employment, her reputation preceded her when she made good a daring escape with her daughter to Italy (because M. Lebrun's position was not threatened, he remained at home). In Florence, after seeing the galleries of classical sculpture and paintings, she was invited by the Grand Duke of Tuscany, brother of Marie Antoinette, to contribute a self-portrait to his collection (FIG. 69). Because she was on the point of leaving the city, she did the work upon arrival in Rome. "I painted myself palette in hand before a canvas on which I was tracing a figure of the Queen in white chalk."[3]

By happy coincidence Vigée-Lebrun and Angelica Kauffmann met while both were in Rome at this time. The two women, among the most distinguished living painters of their respective countries, spent two long evenings together. "I found her," Vigée-Lebrun wrote to the French artist Hubert Robert, "very interesting, apart from her talent, on account of her intelligence and her knowledge. She is a woman of about fifty, very delicate, her health having suffered in consequence of her unhappiness in marrying, in the first instance, an adventurer who had ruined her. She has since married again, to an architect who acts as her man of business."[4]

In Naples Vigée-Lebrun rented a villa by the sea facing toward the island of Capri. Here, in her comfortable new home, with the Russian Ambassador as her closest neighbor, she painted portraits of the royal family and remarked, "The Queen of Naples, without being as pretty as her younger sister the Queen of France, reminded me strongly of her."[5] Both women must have suffered the terrible tension attending the not-yet decided fate of the Queen of France. Also at this time she did four paintings of Emma, the mistress of Sir William Hamilton, the British Ambassador to the Court of Naples whom she officially married the following year. This vivacious young Englishwoman was famous for her creation of "attitudes," a series of poses representing classical figures, and Vigée-Lebrun portrayed her twice as a *Bacchante* and twice as a *Sibyl*. One of the latter paintings was carried by the artist as she moved about in exile, exhibiting it as evidence of her skill. While the style of her royal portraits continued to be in the Rococo manner of her Parisian work, these paintings of the future Lady Hamilton display a more neo-classical tendency.

Hoping to return home, Vigée-Lebrun moved northward back to Turin, but conditions for royalists were still perilous in her homeland. Consequently she postponed her return, traveling instead to Vienna where she leased a small house in Hietzing, a village adjacent to Schoenbrunn park. Her *Memoirs* record that she did a large portrait of Princess Lichtenstein as well as portraits of Princess Esterhazy and many other aristocrats. During this Austrian period she received a disheartened letter from her brother with news of the death by guillotine of her royal patron Marie Antoinette.

Journeying on to St. Petersburg, the French painter was greeted by Catherine II with the following words, "I am delighted, madame, to see you here; your reputation has preceded you. I am fond of the arts and especially of painting. I am not adept but am a fancier."[6] During the artist's six-year sojourn at the Russian court, she saw the Empress die and the succession of her son Paul. The new Czar commissioned his illustrious foreign visitor to paint his wife. Numerous Grand Dukes and Grand Duchesses also sat for their portraits. Vigée-Lebrun's days were spent in working at her easel and her evenings in attending concerts and lavish court balls. On Sundays she interrupted her routine to receive distinguished visitors in her studio. The only blemish on these happy times was her daughter's infatuation with a Russian employed as secretary to a count.[7] Vigée-Lebrun felt that he was too old and too common for her daughter Julie to marry, but the girl resolutely insisted and received consent to the union from her distant (and almost forgotten) father in Paris. The episode humiliated the artist and precipitated her departure from Russia.

On her way home Vigée-Lebrun was intercepted in Berlin by the Queen of Prussia who begged her to travel to Potsdam to do her portrait. After painting several members of the Prussian royal family, she finally reached Paris in 1801. Napoleon was in control, and, since he proffered no official recognition of Vigée-Lebrun, she made what was intended to be a three-month visit to England but stayed three years fulfiling requests for portraits and accepting invitations to the estates of various nobility. Her travels included a stop at the fashionable spa town of Bath, where at the time Jane Austen was living with her family and furtively working away at her novels. The most prominent person whom Vigée-Lebrun portrayed during this English period was the Prince of Wales (later to become King George IV). He came several mornings to her London studio for his sittings, and though he was about forty and according to the artist a little too fat, she made him look handsome and trim in a Hussar uniform. English painters were irked by the Prince's favoring of the French artist, but the damp weather of London soon drove her away, leaving major commissions to the fashionable portraitist, Thomas Lawrence.

On her return to Paris an official command did at last come from Napoleon. He requested a portrait of his youngest sister Carolina who turned out to be a difficult subject, because she kept changing her hair style from sitting to sitting. The completed portrait shows her full-length with her daughter beside her. Later this sister and her husband were to be appointed King and Queen of Naples by Napoleon.

From 1808 to 1809 Vigée-Lebrun visited Switzerland where she painted yet one more celebrity, this time from the literary world, Mme Germaine de Staël (FIG. 75). The artist represented her as Corinne, the Greek poet, as an allusion to her recently published popular novel by the same name. Great must have been Vigée-Lebrun's sympathy for this coarse-featured, brilliant woman, exiled from France at Napoleon's order and yearning only for permission to return to her beloved Paris.

In the next few years Vigée-Lebrun's husband, daughter (who was back in Paris—separated from her husband, true to her mother's forebodings), and brother died. These were losses which she felt keenly and which left her quite alone except for the occasional company of two nieces. She proudly wrote in her *Memoirs* that one of these, Eugénie Lebrun, studied painting and became a portraitist, thus following in her footsteps. She herself had stopped painting, having executed according to her own count about 900 paintings, mostly portraits but also more than 200 landscapes.

Stylistically, Vigée-Lebrun matured during the evanescence of the Rococo. Her courtly manner of painting can be seen in her *Marie Antoinette and her Children* (FIG. 71) with the columned hall of Versailles as a backdrop and in the *Portrait of Marquise de Pezé and Marquise de Rouget with her Two Children* (FIG. 72) with its shimmering mauve highlights on the blue dress of Marquise de Pezé and the feathery trees of the garden setting. Actually Vigée-Lebrun expressed admiration for the realism of Jean-Baptiste Greuze and exhorted her niece to study Greuze's technique as she had done; in a portrait such as that of the landscapist *Hubert Robert* (FIG. 73), Vigée-Lebrun deftly captures the alertness and vivacity of her gray-haired friend. The new movement, Neo-Classicism, appealed to the artist, and in many of her late works she painted her subjects in simple drapery with a minimum of background detail.

Vigée-Lebrun's last few years were divided between an apartment in Paris and a summer home in Louveciennes. She died peacefully in Paris at the age of eighty-seven and according to her wish was buried in the cemetery at Louveciennes under a tombstone decorated with a low-relief sculpture of a palette and brushes. It seems highly appropriate for this painter who had earned her living across Europe to have the symbols of the profession marking her tombstone.

FIG. 70 ELISABETH VIGÉE-LEBRUN, *Portrait of Count Shuvaloff*, 1775

FIG. 71 ELISABETH VIGÉE-LEBRUN, *The Marquise de Pezé and the Marquise de Rouget and her Two Children*, 1787

FIG. 72 ELISABETH VIGÉE-LEBRUN, *Marie Antoinette and her Children*, 1787

FIG. 73 ELISABETH VIGÉE-LEBRUN, *Portrait of Hubert Robert*, 1788

FIG. 74 ELISABETH VIGÉE-LEBRUN, *Angelica Catalani,* 1806

FIG. 75 ELISABETH VIGÉE-LEBRUN, *Portrait of Mme de Staël as Corinne*, 1808

FIG. 76 SARAH PEALE, *Self-Portrait*

13 SARAH PEALE
1800·1885

Recognized by many as the first professional woman painter in America, Sarah Peale, after doing portraits of such statesmen as Lafayette, Daniel Webster, and the first Brazilian ambassador to the United States, left the East Coast in her mid-forties to go West and moved to St. Louis where she remained for thirty years. Although preceded in time by Henrietta Johnson, a pastelist active in South Carolina at the beginning of the eighteenth century, Sarah Peale, portraitist and still-life painter, was the first woman in America to support herself entirely, throughout a long life, by the profession of painting.[1]

Born in Philadelphia in 1800, Sarah Miriam was the youngest daughter of James Peale, an industrious if uninspired painter primarily of miniatures. More glamorous was her uncle, the famous Charles Willson Peale, portraitist of George Washington and the first prominent member of this dynasty of American painters. Charles studied in London under Benjamin West and then settled in Philadelphia where he opened a picture gallery and a natural history museum. The father of a large brood of talented children, he hopefully conferred upon them the names of renowned European painters. His first son was named Raphaelle and his first daughter Angelica Kauffmann, after the Swiss painter whom he had known personally in London. Later sons were modestly given the names Rembrandt, Rubens, and Titian. The daughters who followed were called Sofonisba Anguisciola, Rosalba Carriera,[2] and Sybilla Miriam—thus demonstrating a remarkable knowledge, not generally paralleled today, on Charles's part of women artists of the past.

Following the pattern of her four older sisters and her brother, Sarah Peale initially studied with her father James in Philadelphia. One of the elder daughters, Anna Claypoole, soon joined her father as a miniaturist because his eyesight was failing and the finances for such a sizable family required some boosting. However, Sarah at the age of eighteen wanted to work on canvas rather than follow the family tradition of miniature painting. She visited her older cousin Rembrandt in Baltimore for three months to obtain instruction in oil, returning two years later for more tutelage. Rembrandt Peale was the director of a museum which he had modeled after his father's in Philadelphia, combining a gallery of fine arts with a collection of natural history specimens. Achieving success as a painter in 1822, he turned the museum over to his younger brother Rubens, who immediately organized an "Annual Exhibition" in which Sarah and her sister Anna were invited to show their works. Sarah was represented by two still lifes and a portrait. She dallied long enough in Baltimore to fulfill several portrait commissions and included some of these paintings in the next exhibition of 1823.

In 1825 Sarah settled in Baltimore and remained for twenty years. She advertised herself as having "painting rooms in Peale's Baltimore Museum." When the museum closed in 1829, she found an independent studio for herself. The leading families of the city sat for her, and she successfully completed at least 100 portraits. For one of her commissions, a posthumous portrait of Mayor John Montgomery who had died in 1828, she received $100 from the city of Baltimore.

Among the known but missing portraits by Sarah Peale are those of the Marquis de Lafayette and Thomas G. Wildey, founder in Baltimore of the Order of Oddfellows. In 1877, when she reminisced about Lafayette for a newspaper reporter, Sarah recalled that during his triumphal visit to the United States in late 1824 she addressed a note to him suggesting a sitting in Baltimore. The general answered with a polite letter inviting her to come to Washington as he would be able to give her more time there. When the twenty-five-year-old artist arrived in the capital, Lafayette obliged by sitting for her four times.

Sarah had been in Washington before. She had been taken there twice by her uncle, the first time during the presidency of Madison and the second time during Monroe's administration. Sparkling with youth and dressed in the latest fashion, Sarah Peale conquered Washington society during a New Year's reception at the White House.

From 1841 to 1843 Sarah made several more trips to Washington to paint the portraits of many close associates of President John Tyler: Daniel Webster, Secretary of State, Abel P. Upshur, Secretary of the Navy, Congressman Henry A. Wise of Virginia (FIG. 79), Congressman Caleb Cushing of Massachusetts, and Senator William King of Alabama who was later a distinguished American Minister to France. She also did portraits of the following senators: Dixon H. Lewis ("the fat Senator from Alabama" who weighed 460 pounds[4]) and from Missouri both Lewis Linn and Thomas Hart Benton (FIG. 80), the granduncle of the painter of the same name.

In 1846 Sarah Peale's health was not good, and the following year she accepted an invitation to journey westward to St. Louis. Possibly her friendship with the two senators from Missouri encouraged her decision to make the trip. She found the city enough to her liking to stay for three decades.

Once again she was in demand as portraitist to prominent families. Five paintings of the Benjamin Shore family and five of the Owens family have been located. Newspaper items mention additional paintings, for example, her portrait of Father Theobald Matthew, an Irish "temperance priest" who toured the United States and lent his presence to St. Louis in 1851, and portraits of Dr. J. B. Johnson and General William S. Rosecrans. A St. Louis newspaper of 1849 described her studio as follows:

> We have been much delighted with a visit to the studio of Miss Sarah M. Peale, on Washington Avenue. . . . Miss Peale has completed, or has in the course of completion, the portraits of several ladies and gentlemen of this city, and she has transferred their features to the canvas with an accuracy and life-like expression, that cheats the beholder into the belief that he is looking at the original.[5]

A newspaper account announcing that Sarah Peale was about to return East, reported that recently her skills had been devoted to painting fruit pieces. Indeed, she had been engaged in this type of painting since her youth and had received awards for such work. At the St. Louis Fair of 1859 she won first prize for her depiction of a melon, in 1861 both first and second prizes for *Fruit Painting*, in 1862 second prize for *Fruit* and for *Flowers*, and similar awards for still lifes in 1866 and 1867.

Her style of painting was very similar to that of the rest of the family in both portraiture and still life: a straightforward, austere directness that resulted in a realistic representation of subject. Her distinction is the exquisite treatment given to materials such as lace collars and embroidered shawls.

In 1877 the aging painter decided to rejoin her sisters Margaretta and Anna in Philadelphia. Shortly after her return they died, but indomitable Sarah lived on until 1885 to die serenely at the age of eighty-four. The St. Louis newspaper that described her as she left to return East speculated with maudlin sentimentality upon this woman who had chosen a career over marriage:

> During all these years she has remained wedded to her art, and, it may be added, to nothing else; for with the grace of a medium sized brunette and the expression that beams from a countenance of one who possesses the accomplishments of a lady, united to self-dependence, and firmness of character, it might have been well otherwise. . . .[6]

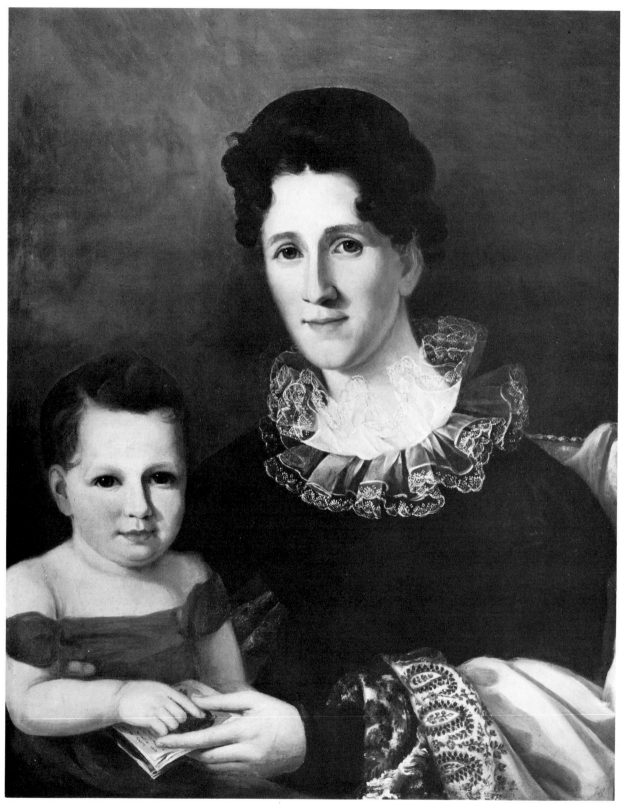

FIG. 77 SARAH PEALE, *Mrs. Ruben Peale and Child*

FIG. 78 SARAH PEALE, *Watermelon*, 1825

FIG. 79 SARAH PEALE, *Portrait of Henry A. Wise*

FIG. 80 SARAH PEALE, *Senator Thomas Hart Benton*

FIG. 81 EDOUARD DUBUFE, *Rosa Bonheur*

14 ROSA BONHEUR
1822·1899

THE FRENCH PAINTER Rosa Bonheur was as independent as she was unconventional. As a child, when apprenticed to a seamstress, she categorically refused to learn such a tame trade and instead successfully argued with her financially strapped but liberally disposed father to let her enter the boarding school in which her younger brothers were already receiving an education. Animals were the favorite subject of her prodigious draftsmanship, and as she grew older and wanted to sketch the lively scenes in the stock yards and the slaughter houses, she simply put on men's clothing to achieve her goal unhampered. Once she discovered the ease of painting and moving about freely in trousers rather than in trailing skirts, Bonheur adopted such attire along with short hair. Earning enough money to travel abroad, she visited England and the Scottish Highlands where she had ample opportunity to paint the wild mountain goats and herds of sheep that roamed the area. Conventional mores were never forced on her by her father, a member of the women's-rights oriented group, the Saint-Simonians, and she admittedly avoided marriage in order to keep her independence. In her thirties she bought a large house in the countryside near Fontainebleau where in addition to a spacious studio she could have a farm to keep the horses and other animals she wanted to paint. Her menage eventually even included a lion. Society accepted and recognized the merit of this confirmed individualist, and she became the first woman artist to be named an Officer in the Legion of Honor.[1]

Rosa Bonheur was born in Bordeaux, a city crowded with Spanish intellectuals and soon to include the painter Goya who chose in 1824 to live there in exile rather than endure the re-imposed Inquisition in Spain. When she was seven, her painter-father, Raymond, moved the family to Paris in the hope of earning more money. Not only did he find it necessary to teach drawing in order to support his growing family, but also his wife was obliged to become a bread-winner by giving piano lessons. Unfortunately her fragile

147

health rapidly gave way, and she died in 1833 leaving the eleven-year-old Rosa, two young sons, and a baby, Juliette. Despite the hardships of poverty all four Bonheur children decided to become artists like their father, working together in the same family studio in which Rosa kept birds and even a sheep as favorite models. The sheep had to live on the balcony of their sixth-floor apartment, and Rosa's brothers would take turns carrying it downstairs when it needed exercise.

Though Rosa spurned the idea of becoming a seamstress to help the family resources, she found to her immense satisfaction that her artistic skills could also produce income. On regular trips to the Louvre, where her father sent her to supplement his lessons at home, she trained herself by making copies of the works of old masters, and before long she discovered a market for her faithful copies. Then at seventeen she became fascinated with the idea of sketching animals outdoors in their natural environment and started making daily trips into the country in search of animals and picturesque landscapes. Horse fairs and cattle markets especially provided her with the subjects she wanted to study. Bonheur began to make small sculptures of oxen, sheep (FIG. 83), and horses. The meticulous realism with which she fashioned her subjects appealed to the public, and bronze casts of her animals were readily sold.

In the Paris Salon of 1841 she exhibited two such sculptural groups, one of rabbits, the other of sheep and goats; both works received favorable notice from art connoisseurs and the public. The next year three of her animal paintings were entered, and these, again because of the extraordinary realism of her style, attracted great attention. She continued to show annually. In the Salon of 1845, in which she was represented by six canvases, Bonheur received a third prize, and her paintings began to command handsome prices.

Her father was appointed director of the government-supported School of Design for Girls in 1848—at 10 rue de Seine in Paris. When he died the following year, Rosa was promoted to the directorship and Juliette served as a resident teacher.

Suddenly that same year Bonheur's career skyrocketed when her painting entitled *Plowing in Nivernais* (FIG. 85) received the Gold Medal in the Salon exhibit and was purchased by the French Government for permanent exhibition in the Louvre. Encouraged by this taste of success the artist decided to create a life-size painting depicting the famous horse market of Paris. Her project (8 × 16½ feet) was reputedly the largest canvas yet attempted by an animal painter (FIG. 84). Some of her many and careful studies for the painting were made at horse auctions and others were made of horses belonging to the equine-powered Paris bus company. Her emancipated mode of dress was certainly suitable as she daily perched on a ladder to work on the immense canvas. The completed painting became the *cause célèbre* at the Salon of 1853. Today it hangs in the Metropolitan Museum dominating the nineteenth century room and continuing to attract attention through its vigorous composition and scintillating white pigments. Because of the extraordinary popularity of the work, Bonheur did a smaller version which is now in the National Gallery, London.

Soon after the Paris success, *The Horse Fair* was exhibited in the major cities of England and was taken at Queen Victoria's request to Buckingham Palace for her private viewing.[2] Bonheur followed her painting across the channel and was enthusiastically received by art patrons and dealers. Scenes of nature were especially popular at this time in an England that could not have enough of John Constable. With the rise of a bourgeois class in England and on the Continent there was a demand everywhere for realistic work similar to Dutch trends of the seventeenth century when the burghers avidly bought landscapes of their countryside to decorate their homes. Bonheur was able to observe that in England the animal painter, Edwin Landseer was enjoying a tremendous popularity, and she returned home with even greater determination to resume her promising career.

She bought an estate in By on the edge of the Forest of Fontainebleau with a studio big enough for both herself and her lifelong friend, Nathalie Micas, to work. At the age of fourteen she had met the frail Nathalie when she was brought by her parents to Raymond Bonheur's studio for a portrait sitting. The girls became close friends, and in their twenties they were sent by the Micas family on a trip to the Pyrenées in hopes that the mountain air might be beneficial for the ailing Nathalie, who also aspired to be a painter. Here at By Rosa kept dogs, horses, sheep, goats, gazelles, bulls, cows, monkeys, a yak, a boar, an eagle, and her by-now-famous lion. The Forest of Fontainebleau provided her with deer and wild boar. During these happy years at By she did many paintings of the animals in the woods as well as of her more domesticated pets.

Empress Eugénie, wife of Napoleon III, visited Bonheur's studio in 1864 to decorate her personally with the Cross of the Legion of Honor. As Bonheur related the occasion to her biographer, "I was in the garden and had just time to change from my masculine clothes. Madam, she told me, I bring you a jewel on behalf of the Emperor. His majesty has authorized me to announce to you your name as chevalier in the imperial order of the Legion of Honor."[3]

The precarious health of Micas necessitated a milder climate, so Bonheur built a villa at Nice where they could spend the winter months. Despite the precautions, Nathalie died in her fifties.

An event which jostled Bonheur out of her mourning was the arrival in France of Buffalo Bill. He had come to Europe with his troup of bronco riders and Indians for the Paris Exposition of 1889. Rosa invited him to By to inspect her horses, and she seized the occasion to paint the Wild-West hero on horseback (FIG. 86). He in turn sent her a gift of two spirited broncos.

An unexpected visit to her studio made in 1898 by Queen Isabella II of Spain caught Rosa wearing blue trousers and a white canvas jacket. However, her penchant for dressing comfortably, which in those days meant in "masculine" attire, was known and understood at home. Sadi Carnot, President of the Republic, made a special request to the painter before visiting her in her studio that she remain in her customary working clothes while showing him her work.

Other honors were bestowed upon Bonheur without personal visits. In 1865 the Emperor Maximilian and Empress Carlotta sent her the Cross of San Carlos from Mexico. The King of Belgium awarded her the Cross of Leopold. Alfonso II of Spain named her a Commander in the Order of Isabella the Catholic, and in 1884 the King of Portugal made her a member of the Order of St. James.

The greatest honor for this Frenchwoman, however, came from being named an Officer in the Legion of Honor. No woman artist before her had been elevated to the rank of officer, and she was justifiably proud to receive this recognition in 1894 from the previous thoughtful visitor to her studio, the President of the Republic.

Bonheur's painting style was only slightly affected by the Impressionist movement that was gaining ascendancy in France during the peak of her career. In her earlier work such as *The Horse Fair* one detects some of the romantic vigor of Gericault's animals, and in the materiality of her pastoral landscapes we see an affinity with her slightly older contemporaries, the members of the Barbizon School. Her particular contribution was her mastery of the anatomy of animals, her accurate observations and plasticity of form, and her empathy for the animals which she portrayed as individualistically as human beings.

In 1899 the seventy-seven-year-old Bonheur, her brown hair now turned completely white, died at By and, as her will specified, was buried in Père-Lachaise cemetery in Paris in the same vault with Nathalie Micas.

Her pioneering way of life was extraordinary for a woman in the nineteenth century: her insistence upon being an artist and not a seamstress, buying her own house in a century which began with women lacking any property rights, wearing unconventional but comfortable clothes, smoking cigarettes, and in general setting her own style instead of accepting the dictates of a tradition-bound society. Here are some of her provocative thoughts on women and civilization as expressed to her biographer:

Why wouldn't I be proud of being a woman? My father, that enthusiastic apostle of humanity, often repeated to me that the mission of woman was to elevate the human race, that she was the Messiah of future centuries. I owe to his doctrines the great and proud ambition that I have conceived for the sex to which I gloriously belong and in which I shall maintain independence until my last day. Besides I am convinced that to us belongs the future; I want to cite two proofs: if Americans walk at the head of modern civilization, it is because of the admirable, intelligent way in which they raise their daughters and the respect they have for their women. On the other hand if the Orientals stagnate in a barbarism from which they cannot disentangle themselves, it is because the husbands do not sufficiently esteem their spouses and by consequence the children are not disposed to prove their affection for their mother.[4]

FIG. 82 ROSA BONHEUR, *The Studio*, drawing, 1867

FIG. 83 ROSA BONHEUR, *Grazing Ewe*, bronze

FIG. 84 ROSA BONHEUR, *The Horse Fair*, 1853

FIG. 85 ROSA BONHEUR, *Plowing in Nivernais,* 1848

FIG. 86 ROSA BONHEUR, *Col. William F. 'Buffalo Bill' Cody*, 1889

FIG. 87 *Edmonia Lewis*

15 EDMONIA LEWIS
1843·?

HALF AMERICAN INDIAN and half American Negro, Edmonia Lewis was raised by her mother's tribe, the Chippewa Indians. Born in Greenhigh, Ohio, in 1843, she later described her parents and nomadic childhood with the following simplicity:

> My mother was a wild Indian and was born in Albany, of copper color and with straight black hair. There she made and sold moccasins. My father, who was a negro, and a gentlemen's servant, saw her and married her ... Mother often left home and wandered with her people, whose habits she could not forget, and thus we, her children, were brought up in the same wild manner. Until I was twelve years old, I led this wandering life, fishing and swimming ... and making moccasins.[1]

During the middle of the last century the state of Ohio was a sympathetic haven for fugitive slaves. The town of Oberlin served as a stop-over on the "underground railroad" to the North and already had a large population of free blacks by the time Oberlin College was founded in 1832. Not only was Oberlin the first institution of higher education in America to open its doors to women, it was also the first school to admit women of all races. Orphaned during her early teens, Edmonia apparently received an Abolitionist scholarship to go to Oberlin College, where she arrived by stagecoach to begin her freshman year in 1856. Her first three years of study went well with traditional academic subjects, such as Greek and Zoology. Although she would like to have taken sculpture, no such course was offered in the liberal arts curriculum.[2] But suddenly in her senior year her two best white friends were poisoned, and Lewis was charged with their murder. Fortunately James Mercer Langston, later to become professor of law at Howard University and the first Negro elected to Congress, was practicing law in Oberlin at this time. A graduate of the college, he took an immediate interest in the case and defended Lewis. The trial ended in acquital, and the relieved girl was triumphantly carried from the courtroom on the shoulders of her friends and fellow students, as related by Langston himself in his autobiography.[3]

Boston, center of liberal thought in the nineteenth century, attracted Lewis, and with a letter of introduction to the anti-slavery advocate William Lloyd Garrison, she traveled there in hopes of pursuing a musical career.[4] But once in the Massachusetts capital she was impressed with the sculptural busts which she saw in the State House and with monuments which decorated the city in honor of early American patriots. She particularly liked the life-size statue of Benjamin Franklin by Richard Greenough which had been recently placed in front of City Hall. Garrison, once aware of her interest, gave Lewis an introduction to the neo-classical sculptor, Edward Brackett, who at their first meeting handed her some clay and a model of a human foot, advising her to go home and begin work. Her progress in the medium was notable, and before long she created her first independent sculpture—a portrait medallion in memory of John Brown, the Abolitionist martyr.

With many other free blacks she witnessed the solidification of opposing views regarding abolition of slavery that divided North from South. After the Civil War broke out in 1861, the black leader Frederick Douglass urged the formation of a Negro regiment to fight against the South, and in response the 54th Massachusetts Regiment was organized. Edmonia Lewis was actually standing in the crowd lining the Boston streets as Colonel Robert Gould Shaw and his black troops of the 54th Massachusetts Regiment paraded through the city to the port for embarkation on 28 May 1862. Flags, streamers, and bunting were up, and reserve policemen were on duty in case of public resentment toward the unusual spectacle of armed black soldiers. They were sent to South Carolina where the following summer Colonel Shaw was killed in battle. Lewis did a bust of the white colonel who was a member of an old Boston Back Bay family and a Harvard graduate. Exhibited at the Soldier's Relief Fair, the bust became so popular a work that 100 plaster replicas of it were sold, providing the artist with enough money to buy a boat ticket to Europe.

Her destination was Rome, the mecca of American sculptors, where she arrived in 1867, two years after the conclusion of the Civil War. William Wetmore Story, whose biography was written by the novelist Henry James, was already there and so was an astonishing number of women sculptors including Harriet Hosmer, Emma Stebbins, Margaret Foley, and Anne Whitney. James refered to these women working in marble as "the white, marmorean flock." "Amazons" might have been a better label for some of them: Harriet Hosmer, at work on a colossal statue of Senator Thomas Hart Benton for which she had to mount a giant scaffolding, was scandalizing the city through her choice of recreation—riding horseback alone through the Roman Campagna. On their visits to Rome the Brownings socialized with the American artists, and in 1854 Elizabeth Barrett Browning wrote:

I should mention, too, Miss Hosmer . . ., the young American sculptress, who is a great pet of mine and of Robert's, and who emancipates the eccentric life of a perfectly 'emancipated female' from all shadow of blame by the purity of hers. She lives here all alone (at twenty-two); dines and breakfasts at the *cafés* precisely as a young man would; works from six o'clock in the morning till night, as a great artist must, and this with an absence of pretention and simplicity of manners which accord rather with the childish dimples in her rosy cheeks than with the broad forehead and high aims.[5]

"Emancipated females" these women sculptors in Rome certainly were. Hosmer and Louisa Lander[6] were the prototypes of the women artists "of free spirit" in Nathaniel Hawthorne's *The Marble Faun* of 1860. American writers who came to Rome made a point of calling on the women sculptors in their studios. Among the distinguished tourists were Herman Melville, Mark Twain, Harriet Beecher Stowe, Longfellow, Edith Wharton, Margaret Fuller, William Dean Howells, Theodore Parker, and the journalist Henrietta Stackpole who came to study the position of Italian women.[7] The Caffè Greco near the Spanish Steps was a frequent gathering place, and everyone's studio was within a short radius.

Lewis moved into a studio near the Piazza Barberini on Via San Niccolo di Tolentino, the same street where W. W. Story had his studio, and not far from Hosmer and others on Via Margutta. She mastered the difficult technique of sculpture, working directly in marble, and created ethnic group studies such as an emancipation work titled *Forever Free* (Howard University Gallery of Art) showing a standing Negro man comforting a kneeling woman, both of whom have broken their chains of bondage. She also chose to illustrate American Indian subjects related to Longfellow's poem *Hiawatha*. A newspaper item in *The Revolution*, datelined Rome, 21 March 1871, describes as follows works seen on a visit to her studio:

Her first *Hiawatha's Wooing* represents Minnehaha seated making a pair of moccasins and Hiawatha by her side with a world of love and longing in his eyes.

In *The Marriage* they stand side by side with clasped hands. In both, the Indian type of features is carefully preserved and every detail of dress, etc., is true to nature; the sentiment is equal to the execution.[8]

Hiawatha's Wooing impressed the American actress Charlotte Cushman so much that she and a group of other Americans bought it and presented it to the Boston YMCA.[9] Cushman was especially helpful to her compatriots abroad, and she had a particular regard for the struggling women sculptors. She was the person responsible for bringing the young Harriet Hosmer from Watertown, Massachusetts, to Rome. She shared her apartment at the head of the Spanish Steps with the sculptor, Emma Stebbins, and when she was back on tour in America she was delighted to read in the New Orleans *Picayune* of 7 January 1873 that "Edmonia Lewis had snared two 50,000 dollar commissions."[10]

Indeed, Lewis's work did sell for large sums and her studio became one of the most fashionable places for tourists to visit. They were fascinated by the contrast of her brown hands working the white marble. The newspaper *The Revolution* describes with the typical aesthetic prejudices of its day what the visitor could hope to see:

> Edmonia Lewis is below the medium height, her complexion and features betray her African origin; her hair is more of the Indian type, black, straight, and abundant. She wears a red cap in her studio, which is very picturesque and effective; her face is a bright, intelligent and expressive one. Her manners are child-like, simple, and most winning and pleasing. She has the proud spirit of her Indian ancestor, and if she has more of the African in her personal appearance, she has more of the Indian in her character.
>
> She is one of the most interesting of our American women artists here, and we are glad to know that she is fast winning fame and fortune.[11]

In addition to her ambitious group sculptures, such as *The Indian Arrowmaker and his Daughter* (FIG. 88), she did portrait busts of Abraham Lincoln (FIG. 90), Henry Wadsworth Longfellow, Wendell Phillips (literary editor of *The Nation*), and Charles Sumner, Senator from Massachusetts. She returned to America in 1873 when five of her works—*Bust of Lincoln, Asleep, Awake* (FIG. 91), *Hiawatha's Marriage*, and *Poor Cupid*—were exhibited in San Francisco. *Poor Cupid* and *Hiawatha's Marriage* were sold immediately, and Lewis then took the remaining three works to nearby San Jose for an exhibit. Newspaper accounts report that over 1600 visitors saw her work, and the San Jose Library canvassed for subscriptions to purchase the Lincoln bust.[12] The other two pieces were privately bought but have now found their way to the same library.

Though information is still scarce on Lewis, she was apparently in Boston in 1885 when her *Forever Free* was presented at Tremont Temple to Reverend

Grimes an advocate of black equality. She seems to have been back in Rome by 15 June 1885 as a signer of a petition drafted by American artists in Rome. Under the leadership of W. W. Story the Americans sent a letter to Congress criticizing the tax being levied on the work of *foreign* artists, protesting that such "protection" was not needed by American artists.[13]

The following year Frederick Douglass and his wife while strolling on the Pincian Hill in Rome noted running into the "oddly dressed" sculptor.[14] The simple, informal clothes of the working artist seem to have disturbed these visitors to Rome who were still accustomed to seeing women in long skirts.

No further record of Lewis appears. In the aftermath of the Civil War a new kind of vigorous artistic expression began to supersede her neo-classicist style. The more realistic bronze sculpture of Saint-Gaudens and Daniel Chester French replaced in popularity the white marble figures in classical drapery of Lewis, Hosmer, Story, and the other expatriate Americans. The quiet drama of *Hagar* (FIG. 92), which had appealed to viewers when it was created in 1875 and about which Lewis commented, "I have a strong sympathy for all women who have struggled and suffered,"[15] seemed to lack the immediacy which was demanded toward the end of the century. Nevertheless, Edmonia Lewis's place in history remains secure as the first black American to receive international recognition as a sculptor.

FIG. 88 EDMONIA LEWIS, *Old Indian Arrowmaker and his Daughter*

FIG. 89 EDMONIA LEWIS, *Hiawatha*, 1868

FIG. 90 EDMONIA LEWIS, *Bust of Abraham Lincoln*, 1870

FIG. 91 EDMONIA LEWIS, *Awake*, 1872

FIG. 92 EDMONIA LEWIS, *Hagar*, 1875

Suzanne Valadon
1883

FIG. 93 SUZANNE VALADON, *Self-Portrait*, 1883

16 SUZANNE VALADON
1865·1938

After the exemplary success of such Impressionist painters as Berthe Morisot, Eva Gonzalès, and Mary Cassatt, it is no surprise that among the Post-Impressionists there should emerge a talented woman artist. What is unexpected, though, is that Suzanne Valadon, who had no formal instruction and who began her professional life as an acrobat in the circus before becoming a model, should succeed as a leading French painter. Also unusual is the fact that we finally come upon a woman who teaches her son—Maurice Utrillo—to become an artist, instead of the customary sequence of a father instructing his daughter or son.

Illegitimately born in the French town of Bessines (near Limoges), the child baptized Marie-Clémentine Valadon was taken within a few months to Paris by her mother, Madeleine Valadon. It was later in her teens that the girl on the urging of her friend Toulouse-Lautrec changed her name to the more colorful "Suzanne."

Madeleine Valadon, who earned her living as a seamstress, settled with her baby in Montmartre, the easy-going Bohemian paradise for impecunious artists on the outskirts of Paris. She found that work in a dress factory was unbearably oppressive and preferred to support herself by scrubbing floors in shops and offices. Madame Valadon's small daughter was left for the day with the concierge of her tenement and later for a brief time was enrolled in the kindergarten classes at the Convent of St. Vincent de Paul. But the Franco–Prussian War of 1870–1871 disrupted all routine, and the six-year-old Suzanne was left free to roam the streets of Montmartre, where she often stopped to watch artists at work before their easels. In the solitude of her room she began to sketch and draw. These early efforts were not taken seriously by her hard-working mother, however, and, when Suzanne reached the age of nine, she was considered old enough to be apprenticed as a dressmaker in a factory. After enduring sweatshop conditions for three years, she left for a series of jobs, as a waitress, a dishwasher, a vegetable vendor in

Les Halles, and a groom in a livery stable.

Finally at sixteen she thought she had found her profession as a circus performer, but an accident abruptly ended this career after only seven months. While substituting for an indisposed trapeze artist, she fell and, although not permanently injured, was forced to find less hazardous work.

An appealing *gamine* with blue eyes and blonde hair, her supple body attracted the professional attention of the artists she liked to watch at work. She was hired as a model by a succession of famous painters beginning with Puvis de Chavannes, the creator of Symbolist murals who, despite his fifty-seven years, fell in love with the seventeen-year-old model. Her evenings were spent with lively friends her own age in the cafés of Montmartre, and in the spring of 1883 she became infatuated with a Catalan student named Miguel Utrillo.[1] Pregnancy soon interrupted Valadon's modeling work, and in December her son Maurice was born. Although it is still a moot question who the father actually was, eight years later Miguel Utrillo offered to sign a legal document giving the boy his surname.[2]

The next artist for whom she worked was Renoir. She posed for a number of his paintings including *Le Bal à Bougival* (Boston Museum of Fine Arts) and the *Bathers* (Philadelphia Museum). In 1887 Toulouse-Lautrec took a studio in the building where Valadon lived with her mother and son, and soon she was also modeling for this caustic but compassionate observer of the Paris scene. When Lautrec discovered that Valadon herself possessed a superb natural talent for drawing, he insisted upon taking her to meet Degas whose artistic judgment he respected. This was the turning point in Valadon's life. Degas greeted her work with enthusiastic praise and not only urged her to become a full-time painter but arranged for her work to be exhibited in several Parisian galleries.

Meanwhile in her personal life Valadon acquired a new lover, the banker Paul Mousis. Enchanted by the gregarious artist, Mousis built a new mansion in a "respectable" section of Paris and persuaded Valadon to come live with him. By this time her son, perhaps from neglect, had taken to drinking and had to be sent to a sanatorium for an alcohol-cure. When the young man returned home to recuperate, Valadon had the inspiration of teaching him to paint. Before long Maurice was copying scenes of Montmartre and was well enough to live alone in his mother's studio which she still retained on Rue Cortot. He made the acquaintance of his first real friend, the painter André Utter. Shortly thereafter Valadon, weary of the bourgeois banking circle, left Mousis and returned to her Montmartre studio to live. The inevitable happened: the young André and the restless, flambuoyant Suzanne fell in love, despite the twenty-one-year gap in their ages. Five years of happiness and productive painting ensued for the couple during which Valadon specialized in scenes of nude figures. The outbreak of World War I interrupted this idyllic period. Precipitated by Utter's being called up to service, the couple dashed to City Hall for a legal marriage—he twenty-eight and she a dynamic forty-nine.

The German invasion of Belgium did not halt art activities in Paris, and in 1915 Valadon had her first solo exhibition at the Berthe Weill Gallery. This was followed by a showing of the "wicked trinity"—Valadon, Utrillo, and Utter—in 1917 at the Bernheim Jeune Gallery. With the signing of the Armistice the art market soared, and these artists were given many more shows. The works of Valadon and Utrillo in particular began to sell, commanding reasonably high prices. In a euphoric state Valadon and Utter explored the countryside around Lyons and, emboldened by their new source of income, bought the Chateau St. Bernard. Here over the following decade she painted many still lifes and landscapes, and had plenty of works ready for the *Women and Flowers Exhibition* of 1929, for a group show with Utrillo and Utter in Geneva, and a one-woman exhibition at the Galeries Georges Petit in 1932. At her St. Bernard country home Valadon entertained lavishly; her guests included Premier Édouard Herriot, the painter André Derain, and the poet Max Jacob. The Chateau St. Bernard also proved to be a haven for Utrillo, who once again was recovering from addiction to alcohol. Valadon lived to see her gifted but tormented son receive the ribbon of the Legion of Honor.

In April of 1938, before reaching her seventy-third birthday, Valadon was at work in her Montmartre studio, painting a bowl of flowers when she had a stroke. She died in the ambulance on the way to the hospital. Herriot, twice Premier of France, delivered the eulogy at her funeral in Montmartre's parish church, St. Pierre.[3]

Her own words could well serve as a eulogy, "Painting for me is inseparable from life. I put to work the same tenacity that I put, less vigorously, to living, and I have seen all painters, who are committed to their métier, proceed with the same application."[4]

Valadon's special forte was the female nude, standing or reclining, outlined in black with sinuous curves which contrast with a patterned fabric or the striped bedclothes of a domestic interior. She readily admitted a respect for Gauguin's painting and went with Degas to the *Exposition Universalle* of 1889 to see Gauguin's latest canvases. Valadon's drawing style over a period of six decades is characterized by a consistency of fluid, elegant contours and an unlabored plasticity of form. Her work finds parallels in the 1880's and 1890's with the Symbolist Pont-Aven school of painters around Gauguin and during the 1920's with the decorative flat designs of Matisse. Simply to place her in the "School of Paris," a safe catch-all phrase for artists working in the French capital early in the twentieth century, does both Valadon's form and content a disservice, for her art carries the domestic and figural aspects of Post-Impressionism well into the third decade of the twentieth century.

By Suzanne Valadon's day the existence of women artists in France was fully accepted and recognized. A year before her death Valadon was able to attend the *Women Painters Exhibition* at the Petit Palais in which representative works from her entire oeuvre were hung.[5] Alongside were paintings by Vigée-Lebrun, Berthe Morisot, Marie Laurencin, and Sonia Terk Delaunay, demonstrating a continuity of women painters in France through three centuries.

FIG. 94 SUZANNE VALADON, *The Circus*, 1889

FIG. 95 SUZANNE VALADON, *Utrillo at his Easel*, 1919

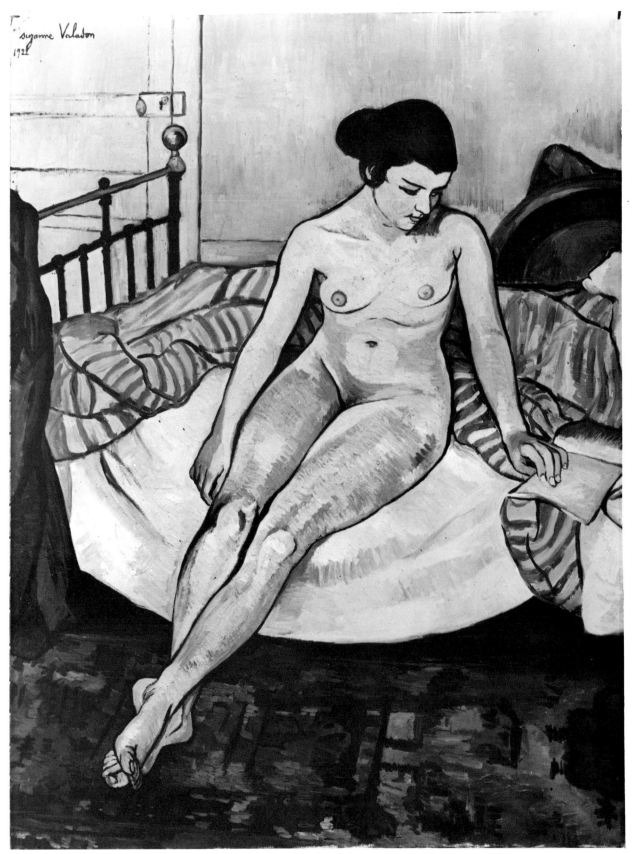

FIG. 96 SUZANNE VALADON, *Nude*, 1922

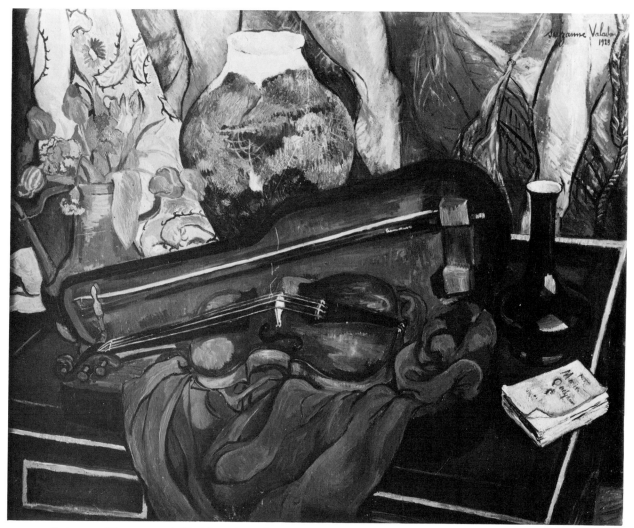

FIG. 97 SUZANNE VALADON, *Still Life with Violin*, 1923

FIG. 98 SUZANNE VALADON, *Church of Saint Bernard in the Trees*, 1929

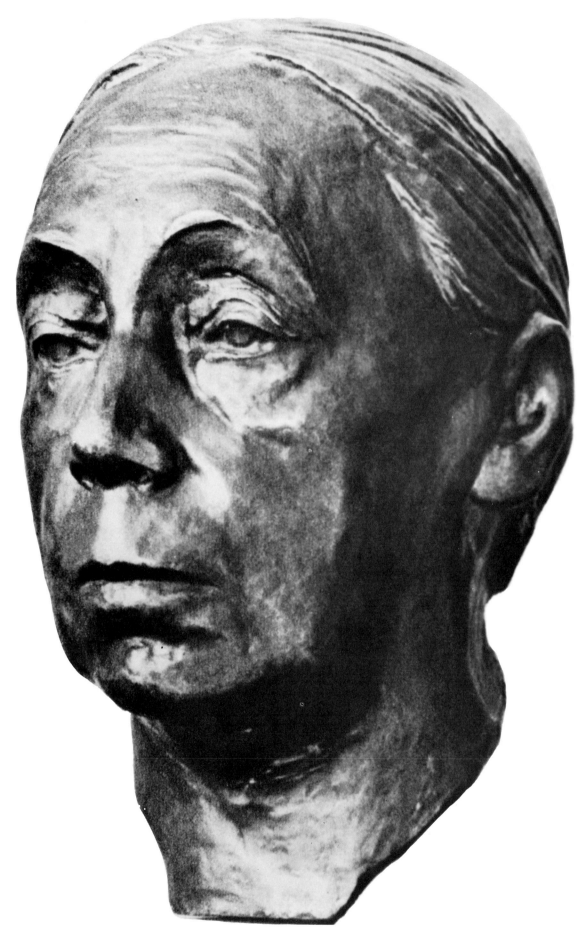

FIG. 99 KÄTHE KOLLWITZ, *Self-Portrait*, bronze, 1936

17   KÄTHE KOLLWITZ 1867·1945

THE GRAVE SOCIAL PROBLEMS of a twice-ravaged Germany during the first half of the twentieth century are strongly reflected in the work of Käthe Kollwitz. She was profoundly disturbed by the plight of the unemployed and by the two World Wars with their concomitant senseless destruction of human lives. In both graphic art and sculpture her deep compassion for humanity is unequivocally expressed.

As the daughter and granddaughter of preachers in the Free Congregation, a new humanistic religion emphasizing ethical rationalism, she was brought up in a liberal and intellectual environment. Her father, Karl Schmidt, encouraged Käthe and her younger sister to become artists, and, after studying with a local engraver, Käthe was sent to the Art School for Girls in Berlin where the Swiss painter Karl Stauffer-Bern was her teacher for a year. On returning to her home in the East Prussian town of Königsberg, she became engaged to a medical student, Karl Kollwitz. However, Käthe's father, fearing that marriage and a career were not compatible, packed her off to the Women's Art School in Munich for two years. In her diary she writes enthusiastically about her gifted classmates and her teacher, Ludwig Herterich, but admits that color was her stumbling block until she read Max Klinger's brochure *Painting and Drawing* which convinced her that themes expressing the darker side of life were more suited to drawing than to painting. This was an important conclusion for the young art student, for she like so many other spokesmen of the melancholy felt more comfortable in the black and white medium of the graphic arts—drawing, lithography, and etching. When Karl completed his medical studies, he was appointed doctor in charge of a socialized health plan for tailors and their families in Berlin, and he urged Käthe to join her future with his. At the age of twenty-three Käthe married Karl and moved to the Prussian capital where she was to live for fifty years. In 1892 she gave birth to her first child Hans, and four years later another son Peter was born.

179

An important stimulus for the development and focus of Kollwitz's social imagery came at this time curiously not from life but from the stage of the Berlin theater in the form of Gerhart Hauptmann's play of 1892, *The Weavers*. This play, ostensibly about the plight and 1840 revolt of Silesian factory workers, was undeniably applicable, in its depiction of social injustice, to the current situation of Berlin's exploited, starving proletariat. The fact that Hauptmann's play was soon closed down by the police confirmed the political implications which the public read into the performances of this, Germany's first social drama. After seeing the controversial play, Kollwitz was spurred to begin a graphic series on the same theme. From among the etchings which follow the march of the weavers to their tragic end, we illustrate here *The Storming of the Owner's House* (FIG. 100), in which the contrast between the ragged knot of rebel workers and the elegant iron gates of the owner's villa is characteristic of the eloquence of Kollwitz's impressive imagery. *The Weavers* was shown in the large Berlin Art Exhibition of 1898, and the jury proposed it for the gold medal, an honor vetoed however by the horrified Kaiser. Nevertheless, when exhibited the next year at Dresden, the series was accorded a gold medal and became known throughout Germany. The success of *The Weavers* resulted in Kollwitz's being invited to teach graphic arts and life drawing at the same Art School for Girls where she had previously been a student.

In her late thirties Kollwitz traveled to Paris and began her first instruction in sculpture. She attended sculpture class at the famous Académie Julian in the mornings and visited museums in the afternoons. Twice she was entertained by Auguste Rodin—in his studios in Paris and Meudon—and was significantly impressed with the monumentality of his great bronze sculptures.

In 1907 Kollwitz provided further proof that her father's fears about combining career and marriage were unjustified by winning the Villa Romana prize, and leaving for a year in Florence. Her younger son accompanied her for the beginning of the stay, and after a walking tour to Rome with an Englishwoman, she was joined by the rest of her small family.

The Italian sojourn reinforced Kollwitz's sculptural ambitions, and upon her return home she began her first independent pieces—mostly single figures or two figures, such as Mother and Child. When World War I broke out, Kollwitz's altruistic concern for humanity was touched by a personal anxiety as her younger son Peter and his friends immediately enlisted, inspired by the idea of sacrifice for the Fatherland. A newspaper article about woman's "joy of sacrificing" provoked Kollwitz to ask in her diary, "Where do all the women who have watched so carefully over their loved ones get the heroism to send them to face the cannon?"[1] Her worst fears were confirmed when Peter was killed on the battlefield in Flanders in October 1914. All the grieving mother could do was to turn her energy into creating a monument for his grave. While working on the ensemble, she wrote of trying to find Peter in her work. Eighteen years later the life-size granite figures of Peter's kneeling mourners, *Father* and *Mother*, both rendered with an almost abstract simplicity, were placed in the cemetery in Belgium. Kollwitz wrote in her diary that she stood in the cemetery before the *Mother*, "looked at her—my own face—and I wept and stroked her cheeks."[2]

Like her artistic counterpart, Ernst Barlach, she had always been opposed to war, and she especially blamed Germany for making young people feel it was their patriotic duty to die for their country. Bitterly, she mused:

> People who would be friends under other conditions now hurl themselves at one another as enemies. Are the young really without judgment? Do they always rush into it as soon as they are called? Without looking closer? Do they rush into war because they want to, because it is in their blood so that they accept without examination whatever reasons for fighting are given to them? Do the young want war?[3]

As the war approached an end in 1918 Kollwitz wrote in a newspaper article, "That these young men whose lives were just beginning should be thrown into the war to die by legions—can this really be justified?"[4]

Two of her most mordant responses to war are the bronze figure groups *Soldiers' Wives Waving Farewell* and *Tower of Mothers* (FIG. 105). A diary entry for 1922 describes the germination of the latter work, "I toy with the thought of doing the mothers standing in a circle defending their children, as sculpture in the round."[5] By the time the work was completed and ready for exhibition, the Nazis were in power and forbade its display, pronouncing, "In the Third Reich mothers have no need to defend their children. The State does that."[6]

Prior to the Nazi takeover, Kollwitz's reputation in Germany was such that an entire room of the Crown Prince Palace in Berlin was devoted to her work, but these pieces were soon relegated to the cellar along with the sculptures of Barlach.[7] Her trouble with the Nazis did not stop there. In the 1930's they forced her to resign her professorship at the Prussian Academy of Art, of which she had been made a full member in 1919, and to give up her spacious studio. Finding an alternative small studio, she composed her last great graphic cycle, eight lithographs on the subject of Death. The theme of death had been a constant preoccupation for Kollwitz, both personally and in her work. As a child she had seen a young brother die and had shared her parents' grief. Death ubiquitously followed her as she suffered the premature demise of her son on the battlefield. With consternation she watched her husband Karl's health give way under the demanding schedule of his charity work, and in 1940 she was left a widow. The blacks in her graphics seemed to increase in volume and value as if in response to the multiple experiences of death, and her figures showed an ever-increasing drastic reduction of form and elimination of detail. Kollwitz had always maintained a will to live after her losses, driven by the wish to fulfill her artistic gift. But in the final years, as her own strength waned, her desire to continue weakened. A further devastating blow was the death on the Russian front of her grandson Peter during the early years of World War II. Torn in her loyalties, she told her granddaughter, "I love Germany deeply and I know that she has a mission. But that mission is not to send eighteen-year-olds into the field of battle."[8]

The Allied bombing of Berlin necessitated Kollwitz's being evacuated to the countryside. There, working very little, she received the news that her home of fifty years had been destroyed. In her seventy-seventh year Käthe Kollwitz passed away under the affectionate care of her son Hans's daughter who read to her at night from the writings of her favorite author, Goethe.

Kollwitz's figurative sculpture always embodies an emotive idea. One of her most severe pieces, laconic in style, eloquent in meaning, is *Lament*, a grieving head which she sculpted as a memorial to her friend Barlach upon his death in 1938. Another is her family gravestone: a relief sculpture of a head resting at peace within the hands of God.

But it is as a graphic artist that she worked consistently throughout her long professional life with a complete mastery of the various techniques and with an intrepid exploration of new combinations to achieve special textural qualities in order to emphasize better the universal content of her radically simplified formal language. Like Kokoschka, she responded to social disasters. When general starvation threatened Vienna in 1920, Kollwitz quickly made a poster for the Austrian aid program: *Vienna is Dying! Save its Children!* (FIG. 102), and, when post-war inflation caused widespread hunger among the working-class families in Germany, she designed the poster entitled *Bread!* to raise money for the strikers. The image in *Bread!* is direct, immediate, and simple—two children tug at their mother's dress begging for food. In her diary she testified, "I feel that I have no right to withdraw from the responsibility of being an advocate. It is my duty to voice the sufferings of men, the never-ending sufferings heaped mountain-high."[9] Of her pacifism, exemplified in such placards as her famous post-World War I lithograph, *Never Again War!* (FIG. 104), she said, "It is a new idea, the idea of human brotherhood."[10] This message, repeatedly conveyed in her art, is the keystone of the enduring quality of her work.

FIG. 100 KÄTHE KOLLWITZ, *The Storming of the Owner's House*, etching, 1897

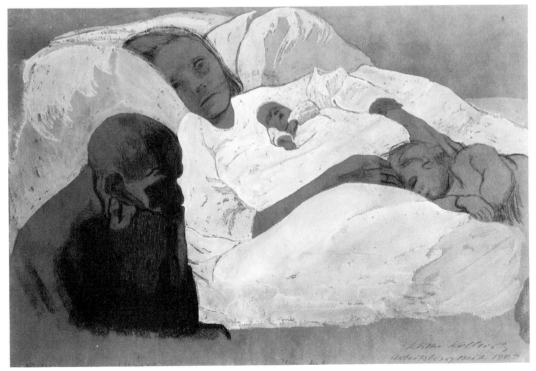

FIG. 101 KÄTHE KOLLWITZ, *Unemployment*, drawing, 1909

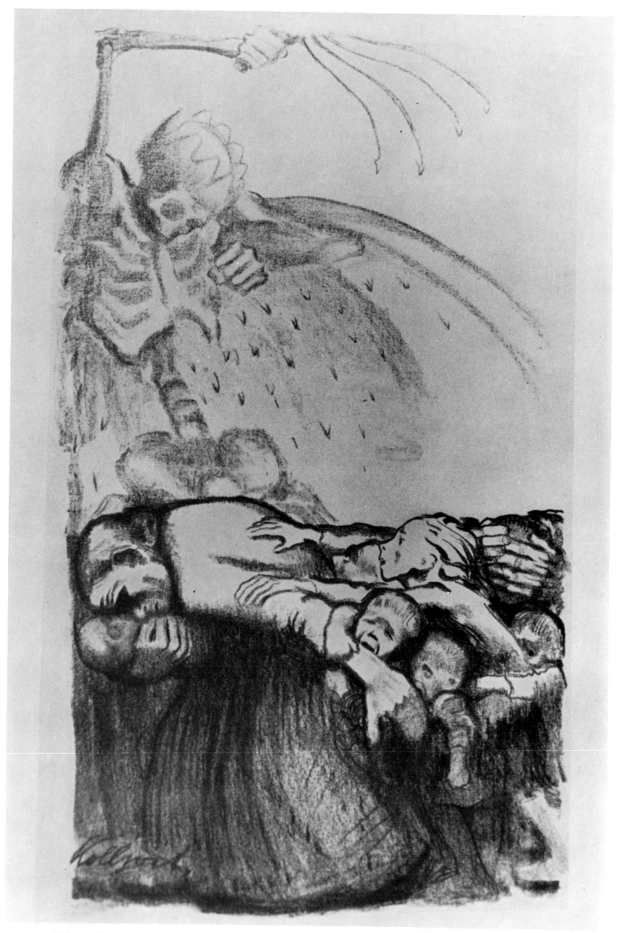

FIG. 102 KÄTHE KOLLWITZ, *Vienna is Dying! Save its Children!*, lithograph, 1920

FIG. 103 KÄTHE KOLLWITZ, *Killed in Action*, lithograph, 1921

FIG. 104 KÄTHE KOLLWITZ, *Never Again War!*, lithograph, 1924

FIG. 105 KÄTHE KOLLWITZ, *Tower of Mothers*, bronze, 1937

FIG. 106 PAULA MODERSOHN-BECKER, *Self-Portrait*, 1906

18 PAULA MODERSOHN-BECKER
1876·1907

THE SUBJECT MATTER of Paula Moder-sohn-Becker's dignified, sober canvases is primarily the human figure—frequently peasant women with wizened, unquestioning faces, young mothers absorbed in their babies, and children dwarfed by chairs or the stalks of flowers. The arresting simplicity of composition, boldness of color and form, and the earnest compassion that emanate from her pictures are reminiscent of Van Gogh, an artist twenty years her senior, and, as with Van Gogh, Modersohn-Becker may be considered as a precursor of the German Expressionist movement. Like Van Gogh, she was an artist whose actual painting career lasted only ten years before a premature death in the thirties, but unlike the Dutch artist she knew from the beginning that she wanted to become a painter.

Her parents tried to direct her into teaching, but Paula Becker was resolutely determined to study art. Her father, an official of the German railroad, had been transferred from Dresden, where Paula was born, to the busy port city of Bremen when she was twelve years old. The family solution to the conflict of interests between the two generations was to permit Paula to study painting for a specified period if she would then promise to enroll in Bremen's Teachers' Seminary. Thus, at sixteen the aspiring artist was allowed to study at the School of Art in London, staying under the protective wing of relatives before entering the two-year teachers' program in Bremen. Once fulfilling this requirement, she persuaded her parents to let her move to Berlin, where more family relatives were on hand, in order to renew her study of art. Letters to her parents during this period make frequent reference to the great strength and feeling of contentment that the act of drawing and painting gave her.

The decisive point in Paula Becker's life occured in the summer of 1897 when, back home in Bremen, she visited nearby Worpswede, a village laced with canals and encircled by birch trees. This bucolic community of thatched-

189

roofed houses on the moors outside Bremen had recently attracted a group of articulate writers and painters yearning for an escape from industrialization and in search of a return to nature. After a short sketching trip in Norway, Paula settled down in the Worpswede artists' colony, choosing to study with its founder, Fritz Mackensen, whose principal motif was the human figure. For the other painters in the movement, Otto Modersohn, Fritz Overbeck, and Hans am Ende, the favorite subject matter was the lonely landscape. Heinrich Vogeler also painted the landscape but he inhabited it with neo-medieval figures from romantic literature. What especially appealed to Paula Becker were the solitary peasant women and children of the village.

On Sundays the artists of the colony would gather for a social evening at Vogeler's. Their fascination with the primitive aspect of life in Worpswede was enhanced by an appreciation of folk art and folk music, and a highlight of the evening was Vogeler's rendition of Negro spirituals on his guitar. In addition to the painters in the group was the sculptor Clara Westoff who bicycled over from her family home in a neighboring town. Often they were also joined by writers, the most distinguished being Rainer Maria Rilke (FIG. 110) whose two recent trips to the Russian hinterlands in search of a "universal" folk spirit made him a sympathetic ally to the Worpswede cause. Rilke's diary testifies to the stimulating discussions and the conviviality of these parties which lasted long into the night in Vogeler's white music-room, and of his attraction for both the "fair-haired painter" and the "sculptress in all her dark vivacity."[1] He spent considerable time visiting Paula's studio, which he described as containing a mask of Dante, a guitar resting against a pile of sketches, and a lily in a vase, and they talked at length about aesthetic and philosophical problems. She asserted that she wanted no God outside the Great Mother, Nature, the giver of life.

Another visitor was the writer Carl Hauptmann, elder brother of the dramatist Gerhart Hauptmann, and one day the whole group set off by carriage for Hamburg to attend the première of Carl's own play. Rilke sat opposite Paula, who was wearing a large hat "on which tired dark red roses unemphatically rested, as if they had just been laid aside by a lonely hand," and as he watched her, he observed to himself that her eyes were beginning to unfold "like double roses."[2] That evening he wrote the prose-poem *Fragment* in which the suitor of a dead, virginal girl lays two red rosebuds on her eyelids and watches in wonderment as the flowers bloom. Rilke's literary fantasy was prophetic, for Paula had less than a decade left to live. In fact, in her own diary she wrote:

. . . I know I shall not live very long. But why should this be sad? Is a feast more beautiful for lasting longer? For my life is a feast, a short intensive feast. My sensual perception grows sharper, as though I were supposed to take in everything within the few years that will be offered me. . . . And if now love also will blossom for me, before I leave, and if I shall have painted three good pictures, I shall leave willingly, with flowers in my hands and in my hair.[3]

Within a year's time Paula Becker had enough paintings ready for her first exhibition which took place in 1899 at the Bremen Art Museum. The critical reaction to her primitivizing line and flat composition was hostile and devastatingly sarcastic, prompting her apprehensive parents to recommend that she give up painting and become a governess. Although disappointed Paula was undeterred. Her belief that she had her own artistic path to pursue had been strengthened by the solidarity of the Worpswede experience, and she determined to see for herself the avant-garde work being done in Paris. Clara Westoff was already there, studying in the sculpture school founded and infrequently visited by the great Rodin, and Paula seized the opportunity to join her. She studied anatomy at the École des Beaux-Arts, made numerous visits to the Louvre where the "beautiful, earnest Holbein portraits" impressed her, attended an exhibition of Cézanne's paintings at Vollard's gallery, and expressed the opinion that Degas turned out entirely too many ballet dancers and absinthe drinkers. She also felt that Degas worked too hard at obtaining "the naïve in line"—a goal towards which her own experiments were pointing.

On returning to Worpswede, Paula accepted the proposal of the recently-widowed Otto Modersohn, and after a carefully-guarded secret engagement they married in 1901. That same year Rilke and Clara Westoff were married and moved to a farmhouse in the nearby village of Westerwede.

After her Paris sojourn Modersohn-Becker's work showed a new monumentality and self-confidence. She concentrated on half-length portraits, emphasizing solemn physiognomies, simplifying the planes of the figures, and minimizing the backgrounds. Her painter-husband confided to his diary in pleased awe, ". . . she is really a great painter. She already paints today better than Vogeler and Mackensen. And my judgment is not at all dictated by love as her family thinks. . . . In her intimacy she is monumental . . . she has a splendid sense of color and of form . . . she has something quite rare. No one knows her, no one esteems her. This will all be quite different some day."[4]

In 1903 Paula made a second protracted trip to Paris, this time studying at the Académie Julian and looking at the paintings of Maurice Denis and the other Breton symbolists whose primitivist tendencies were related to her own. Rilke at this time was serving as personal secretary to Rodin and gave Modersohn-Becker a letter of introduction to the famous sculptor, calling her the wife of a very distinguished German painter. Ironically today *she* is the distinguished painter whose work is preserved in a national museum named after her in Bremen, while her husband's Worpswede canal and birch scenes have slipped into oblivion. Paula may have been too modest about her work, and as a woman she was not taken seriously even by her Worpswede colleagues—a fact about which her husband complained in his diary. Even Rilke in his 1903 illustrated monograph on Worpswede dealt only with the five male artists of the colony.[5]

The next few years indicate a restlessness in Paula as she divided her time between Worpswede and Paris. Otto had the care of his daughter Elsbeth (FIG. 108), born of his first marriage, and was content to remain in the village except for short trips, but Paula thrived on opening her eyes to new stimuli and developments in the art world. In Paris she was able to see some of the latest paintings by Gauguin which encouraged her to continue her own radical color chords and simplification of form. In 1906 she and Otto had an exhibition together in the Bremen Kunsthalle, but again her startling new style was not appreciated. Impressionism appealed more to the public.

While in Paris on her fourth trip in 1907 she was joined by Otto, and they returned to Worpswede together, where on their sixth wedding anniversary Paula recorded the occasion with a *Self-Portrait* showing herself nude and pregnant. After a difficult delivery she gave birth to a daughter, Mathilde, early in November of 1907. But her health had been severely undermined by the event, and before the month was out she died of a heart attack.

Rilke wrote a *Requiem* for his friend in which he refers to the *Self-Portrait* illustrated here (FIG. 106), but a poem written by Paula herself is perhaps a more fitting expression of the rare spirit that for a brief decade illuminated some of the universal constants revealed in the quiet intimacy of Worpswede:

> I feel as if I sat within eternity
> And my soul hardly dared to breathe,
> With tightly closed wings it sits
> And listens, wide-eyed, into the universe.
> And over me comes a soft mildness,
> And over me comes a great strength,
> As if I wanted to kiss white flower petals
> And, beside great warriors, fight great battles.
> And I awaken, trembling with wonder . . .
> So small, you child of man! And yet so enormous

The waves that kiss your soul.
I listen in the dark corner of my room,
Like large, quiet eyes things look back at me
Like large, soft hands that stroke my head.
And blessing flows through every fiber of my being.
That is the peace, dwelling here with me . . .
At my side my lamp burns reliably,
Purrs on its song of life as if in a dream.
Out of the twilight white flowers glisten,
They tremble, shudder, for they sense the future.
With light wingbeat the bat circles my couch
And my soul looks at life's riddle,
Trembles and is silent and looks.
And beside my couch the lamp hums
Its life's song.[6]

FIG. 107 PAULA MODERSOHN-BECKER, *Old Peasant Woman*, 1904

FIG. 108 PAULA MODERSOHN-BECKER, *Elsbeth*, 1902

FIG. 109 PAULA MODERSOHN-BECKER,
Girl Among Birch Trees, 1905

FIG. 110 PAULA MODERSOHN-BECKER, *Portrait of Rainer Maria Rilke*

FIG. III PAULA MODERSOHN-BECKER, *Still Life with Flowers*, 1907

FIG. 112 GWEN JOHN, *Self-Portrait*

GWENDOLEN JOHN
1876·1939

IN A BURST of sibling enthusiasm, the English painter Augustus John called his sister Gwendolen "the greatest woman artist of her age or of any other."[1] The Arts Council of Great Britain, during a retrospective exhibition of her work in 1968, made the judgment that she had produced "some of the finest work by any British artist of the time."[2] And yet today she is scarcely known either in England, or abroad, primarily because her personal subject matter and her intimate, fragile style did not lend themselves to the public taste.

Gwen John and her brother grew up in Pembrokeshire, the most westerly province of Wales. Their birthplace was Haverfordwest, not too far from where the poet Dylan Thomas, whose portrait was later painted by Augustus John, was born a few decades later. The eldest child in the family, Thornton, was followed by Gwen, then Augustus born eighteen months later, and the youngest, Winifred. When Gwen was seven, her mother died, leaving the children in the care of their father, a busy lawyer, and two aunts who quickly assumed the roles of surrogate-mothers. But according to Augustus's autobiography their efforts were not entirely appreciated as both women were proselytizing members of the Salvation Army.[3]

In the summer the family moved to the shore of St. George's Channel which separates Wales from Ireland. There Gwen and Augustus often watched while artists set up their easels and caught the panoramic beauty of the sea resort, Broad Haven. Yet even on vacations the aunts began the family's day with prayers, and soon their over-zealous attention became intolerable for the children's father, who precipitately moved his entire young brood to Tenby on Carmarthen Bay, taking a spacious old house near the seafront.[4]

By this time both Gwen and Augustus had begun to imitate the holiday beach painters and shared a lively interest in portraying the town children:

My sister was always coming across beautiful children to draw and adore. Jimmy was a boy of about twelve when we met him. He wore auburn corkscrew curls down to his shoulders, and his costume was of old green velvet. His face was rather pale and beautiful. . . . Soon we made friends with Jimmy and invited him to our house to be drawn and painted. His mother would come too. Our father didn't approve of these strollers but, as usual, had to give way before our insistence. Our studio was an attic under the roof.[5]

Gwen in her youth was characterized by her brother as being full of high spirits and having a good sense of humor, though occasionally Augustus found her to be both implacable and fiercely intransigent. This is not difficult to understand for, as a young woman eager for formal schooling, Gwen had to sit by and watch her younger brother go off to private school and then to the Slade School of Art at the University of London. Her "implacable" nature paid off, however, and in 1895 she too was allowed by her father to enter the Slade School for an intensive three-year program.

Instruction began with the study of classical sculpture. Once the student acquired sufficient skill drawing from these models, he or she was promoted to the Life Room for drawing and eventually painting before professional models. The same year that Gwen arrived, Henry Tonks was appointed instructor of figure drawing. He had been trained in medicine and served as a demonstrator of anatomy at London Hospital. His impressionist style was quickly absorbed by both Augustus and Gwen John who during this period shared rooms "subsisting, like monkeys, on a diet of fruit and nuts."[6] Augustus remarks that Gwen was not alone as a female student at Slade, for it abounded in talented women students, among whom were Gwen Salmond, Edna Waugh, Ursula Tyrwhitt, and Ida Nettleship (the latter became his first wife).

Both Gwen and Augustus felt very strongly the call to France, and upon completing their studies at Slade, they made their separate ways across the English Channel. While Augustus, buoyed with the success of a one-man show, joined his Slade friends at Etretat on the coast of Normandy, Gwen traveled with her classmates Salmond and Nettleship to Paris where they took a studio apartment together. Gwen wanted to continue her training and enrolled as an afternoon student in the life classes at Whistler's "Academy" which was run by one of his former models, Mme Carmen Rossi. Whistler used to drop in once a week to give the students a critique of their work. Gwen pioneered by inventing her own "methodicity:" a special formula for preparing her canvases, as well as a system of numbering her color mixtures, a scheme so recondite that it remained unintelligible to others. One day when

Whistler encountered Augustus John in the Louvre, he conveyed his greetings to Gwen, and Augustus commented that he thought Gwen's drawings showed a feeling for character. "'Character?' replied Whistler, 'Character? What's that? It's *tone* that matters. Your sister has a fine sense of *tone.*'"[7] Indeed she did possess a restrained, muted sense of color and composed her paintings in the best Whistlerian manner, giving prime importance to the placement of the figure in a tonal setting. Unlike Whistler, however, she also conveyed the character of her sitters through an intensive scrutiny of their faces.

When she returned to London in 1900, at the age of twenty-four, she began exhibiting with the New English Art Club, an organization that had been formed fifteen years earlier by a group of rebellious young artists whose anti-academic work introduced Impressionism into England. Gwen John's paintings were shown there at irregular intervals for the next decade, but her brother has pointed out that she rarely and with reluctance sold her work and then only at a price below what her clients would pay.[8]

After three financially unsuccessful years she left again for the Continent. Her traveling companion this time was another young artist, Dorelia McNeill (FIG. 113), whom Augustus was to marry after the death of his first wife. They took a boat to Bordeaux and from there walked to Toulouse, spending their first night in a field. Hoping to earn enough money to continue on to Italy, they rented two humble rooms in Toulouse and lived on a spartan diet. Their income came from making portrait sketches for three francs each in the local cafés. Dorelia described Gwen at that time as reserved and soft-spoken, pale and oval-faced, her hair something in color between mouse and honey, done with a big bow on top; a slender figure with tiny, delicate hands and feet, yet of exceptional strength, able to carry heavy burdens over long distances; and, while not unsociable, preferring solitude. In a letter her future sister-in-law elaborated further:

> ... You asked me how Gwen dressed and though I cannot remember what she wore she always managed to look elegant, and though I cannot remember what we talked about I do remember some very light-hearted evenings over a bottle of wine and a bowl of soup. ... She much appreciated the good food and wine to be had in that part of France, though we mostly lived on stolen grapes and bread.[9]

Dorelia and Gwen had originally planned to make a walking tour of Italy, but they gave up this idea and stayed three months in Toulouse before Gwen settled in Paris, having decided to make France her residence for the rest of her life. She took a small apartment in Montparnasse and concentrated ex-

201

clusively on painting. Ironically, it was as a model, not as a painter, that she earned her living in those days. Her style became increasingly refined: quiet studies of a single female figure in an interior setting. Generally the figure formed a delicate dark silhouette against a sparkling sunlit wall, or sometimes the effect was reversed and the impasto appeared on the figure set against a flat monochromatic background. The lure of the sea, stamped upon her since childhood, prompted her to make occasional excursions to Brittany. On these trips Gwen sketched her fellow train passengers and painted landscapes, but she was very critical of her own work and destroyed the paintings which did not meet her standard of perfection. Meanwhile her gregarious brother had taken a post as professor of painting at Liverpool University.

At the age of thirty in 1906 she formed a cordial friendship with Rodin who was then sixty-six. His letters to her express his appreciation of her painting and drawing and also his concern for her health which he felt she neglected. Rodin protested that her drab apartment on Rue Ste Placide was too humid and lacked sun. He engaged her to pose for his Whistler monument—a colossal female figure holding a medallion of the artist's portrait—to be placed on the Embankment in London. Although subscriptions for a replica of the work had already been collected in Lowell, Massachusetts, Whistler's birthplace, the actual monument was never completed. Today the study, a two-foot high nude bronze, for which the slender Gwen posed, can be seen in the Rodin Museum in Paris, and a maquette for the work can be studied in the Library of Congress, Washington.

Shortly before Rilke's break with Rodin in 1906, Gwen met the peripatetic poet and became a close friend. For many years they corresponded. A letter from him of 17 July 1908 offers her books, and her letter of April 1927 says, "I accept to suffer always, but Rilke! hold my hand! . . . Teach me, inspire me.. . . . Take care of me when my mind is asleep. You began to help me. You must continue."[10] She had embarked on a metaphysical search which climaxed in her conversion to Catholicism in 1913, and in her move to suburban Meudon where she was able to converse with the Thomist writer, Jacques Maritain, and to visit Rodin in his home. Among the papers found in Gwen's garret apartment after her death were many copies of prayers and meditations, as well as scraps of paper on which she scribbled notes about painting. To a neighbor she commented, "My religion and my art, they are all my life."[11] She went to mass daily and even sketched in church. Among her painting subjects were her new friends, the Dominican Sisters of the Presentation (FIG. 117). In her late work she began to apply her pigment in thick swatches, producing a crusty impasto and a looser, freer construction of the human figure. Occasionally the Meudon landscape attracted her attention, but much of her time was spent doing pen or gouache drawings of people, flowers, and cats. And, as occurs so frequently with lonely people, cats became her faithful companions. Her brother wrote that her move from an attic apartment to a dilapidated shed on a half-acre of wasteland was motivated by her solicitude for her cats and that these beloved animals prevented her coming to England on account of quarantine regulations. But she enjoyed the trees and shrubs that gave privacy to her new "studio," purchased in 1927 with income derived from her one-woman show at the Chenil Galleries in London the year before, and Gwen felt that her brother was being too "bourgeois" in freting about her primitive living conditions. In a letter to Augustus she wrote:

> I told you in a letter long ago that I am happy. When illness or death do not intervene, I am. Not many people can say as much. I do not lead a subterranean life (my subterranean life was in Howland Street). Even in respect to numbers I know and see many more people than I ever have.... It was in London I saw nobody. If in a café I gave you the impression that I am too much alone, it was an accident. I was thinking of you and your friends and that I should like to go to spectacles and cafés with you often. If to 'return to life' is to live as I did in London, merci Monsieur: There are people like plants who cannot flourish in the cold, and I want to flourish. Excuse the length and composition of this letter. It is from a little animal groping in the dark.... When you want to paint me you had better name a time to come and see me in several clothes—I have two hats for instance.[12]

What a pathetic picture she draws of herself—leading the life of an almost complete recluse—but then closing with the proud remark that she owned at least two hats! The scraps of paper found in her studio indicate that she had great confidence in her talent, and indeed in her self-portraits she conveys an obvious strength and single-mindedness of purpose. Not only in her self-portraits but also in her paintings and drawings of others she characteristically shows the sitter absorbed in thoughtful introspection, quietly posed before an undistracting backdrop. Her style by this time had evolved into a post-impressionism along the "Intimist" lines of Vuillard and Bonnard with the psychological overtones of Edvard Munch and the pasty pigments of James Ensor. The flambuoyant Augustus, meanwhile, had given up painting gypsies and traveling in their caravans, and was now enjoying financial success as a fashionable portrait painter and respectability as a full member of the Royal Academy.[13]

In the fall of 1939 at the age of sixty-three Gwen John felt ill and experienced a sudden longing for the sea. She took the train to Dieppe but collapsed on arrival and was taken to the hospital of a religious house where she died. She had neglected to take any luggage with her, but had not forgotten to make provision for her cats in a will. Her legacy to us is twofold: (1) a small oeuvre of paintings, rich in nuance, plus a collection of figural drawings, trenchant in characterization, and (2) the example of an unswerving dedication to art through six decades of slight public recognition.

FIG. 113 GWEN JOHN, *Dorelia in a Black Dress*

FIG. 114 GWEN JOHN, *Nude Girl*

FIG. 115 GWEN JOHN, *A Corner of the Artist's Room in Paris*, 1907–1909

FIG. 116 GWEN JOHN. *Woman Reading at a Window*, 1911

FIG. 117 GWEN JOHN, *The Nun*

FIG. 118 *Massine, Goncharova, Larionov, Stravinsky, and Bakst at Ouchy*, 1915

20 NATALIA GONCHAROVA
1881·1962

AMONG THE PIONEERS of modern art in Russia at the beginning of the twentieth century, the inseparable team of Natalia Goncharova and Mikhail Larionov is internationally famous for having created the Rayonnist movement—an abstract offshoot of Cubism. But Goncharova and Larionov are not only known abroad as innovating painters, but also as stage designers who realized brilliant careers in Paris. Their bold new compositions and exotic use of "Eastern" colors contributed to the spectacular appeal of Diaghilev's Ballet Russe, the first modern ballet company in our century.

Goncharova was born at Ladyzhino near Tula, south of Moscow, in 1881, the same year as Picasso and Larionov. Her family, impoverished aristocratic landowners, had a history of cultural involvement—her mother's relatives had long been patrons of music and her father, an architect, continued a family tradition which went back to the time of Peter the Great. In 1831 an earlier Natalia Goncharova had married the poet Pushkin.[1]

Despite reduced financial means, the family sent Goncharova to high school in Moscow and then to the College of Painting, Sculpture, and Architecture where she trained as a sculptor under Paul Trubetskoy from 1898 to 1902. One day, while modeling from animals at the city zoo, she met Larionov, who turned out to be a fellow student at the College, and a relationship began which was to last a lifetime, although they did not take the trouble to marry officially until their seventies.

These were years of artistic ferment in Russia in which both new and old modes of representation underwent experiment. Native arts such as icons and peasant crafts were being re-evaluated; icons which had been accepted simply as objects of worship in churches were now being studied as works of art. In the 1890's a group of young artists eager to stimulate interest in their national heritage and hoping to initiate a productive exchange of ideas with the West launched a magazine known as *The World of Art*.[2] Serge Diaghilev, who was finishing his studies at St. Petersburg University, became editor of the new magazine in 1898.

On her own Goncharova took up painting and began experimenting with the new styles recently developed in Western Europe, Impressionism and Pointillism. Her still lifes and rural landscapes were shown in a special exhibition of Russian paintings arranged by Diaghilev at the *Salon d'Automne* in Paris in 1906, an occasion which enabled Larinov (Goncharova stayed home) to make his first trip to the French capital. Thus introduced to the bright colors of Fauvism, these two Russian artists were encouraged to continue their own exploration of radical color harmonies. Goncharova painted village scenes, such as *Spring Gardening* (FIG. 119), which were rendered in the simplified planes of Post-Impressionism with flat decorative surface designs and rich vibrant pigments. In 1908 Larionov organized the first *Golden Fleece* exhibition, in which contemporary French and Russian work was shown to the Moscow public. Larionov and Goncharova emerged as the leaders of a new avant-garde, and by their third exhibition, Primitivism derived from folk art had become the principal element in their work.[3]

A group of students expelled from the Moscow College of Painting for "leftish tendencies" exhibited with Goncharova and Larionov in the *Jack of Diamonds* show in 1910, and this historic occasion brought them in touch with Kasimir Malevich, who was later to promulgate another new movement, Suprematism. Malevich was forcefully impressed with Goncharova's paintings and began his own series of stylized "peasant" works.

In 1912 Larionov arranged an ambitious exhibition called *The Donkey's Tail* which included works by Vladimir Tatlin, thus uniting for the first time the four leading figures of Russian modernism—Goncharova, Larionov, Malevich, and Tatlin. Tatlin discovered icon painting through Goncharova, who because of her family's aristocratic ties had access to many private collections. This appreciation for icons, seemingly so akin to the artists' own aims in pictorial directness, resulted in an important public exhibition of the objects, in which, at the urging of Russia's modern painters, old paintings and icons were elevated to the status of national heritage.[4] In this same year of 1912 a contingent of modern Russian paintings was included in a Post-Impressionist exhibition in London. Because her name was spelled "Goncharoff," the assumption was myopically made that the painter must be male.

By now Goncharova's style presented an interesting and personally distinctive blend of the latest Cubist fractionizing techniques with her native traditions of icons and peasant designs. Larionov, more given to abstract speculation than Goncharova, invented his own version of Cubism which he entitled Rayonism, and which involved a breaking up of landscapes and figures into patterns composed of spots and "ray"-lines. The artists collaborated in further developing the new style, and in 1913 they published a Rayonnist Manifesto.

The first one-woman show of Goncharova's work took place in Moscow in 1913, and her Rayonnist painting, *Cats* (FIG. 121), was among the 716 paintings exhibited.[5] Her friend Diaghilev commented that year:

> The most celebrated of these advanced painters is a woman. She has recently exhibited seven hundred canvases representing 'light' and several panels measuring forty square meters. As she has a very small studio she paints them in pieces, by calculation and only sees the whole assembled at the exhibition. This woman has all St. Petersburg and all Moscow at her feet. And you will be interested to know that she has imitators not only of her paintings, but of her person. She has started a fashion of nightdress-frocks in black and white, blue and orange. But that is nothing. She has painted *flowers on her face*. And soon the nobility and Bohemia will be driving out in sledges, with horses and houses drawn and painted on their cheeks, foreheads and necks.[6]

That the "flower tatooing" Goncharova was a prodigious worker is evidenced by the phenomenal number of paintings which she had ready for this first retrospective. Igor Stravinsky was later to remark that he thought Larionov was lazy and that Goncharova did his work for him,[7] but actually in these years the team's male partner was also a dynamo, and it was due to his organizational talents that so many of the early exhibitions took place.

Stylistically the two painters differed discernibly in their work. Larionov's theoretical experiments led him into analytical abstractions of muted colors, whereas Goncharova was more interested in the thematic concerns of Futurism: conveying the sensations of speed and machine animation which she represented in brilliant colors in such paintings as *The Cyclist*, *The Railway Station*, *The Factory*, and *The Electrical Ornament*.[8]

Theatrical design began to catch Goncharova's imagination in 1913, the year in which she also ventured into book illustration, in each case irrevocably breaking through conventional barriers with her daring new formats and intense "primitive" colors. Her latest activities came to the attention of Diaghilev who was then organizing the Ballet Russe in Paris, and in 1914 he called together the best Russian talent he could for a production of *Le Coq d'Or* with costumes (FIG. 122), sets, and curtain by Goncharova, and choreography by Michel Fokine. In his *Memoirs* Fokine vividly recalls his first meeting with Goncharova and Larionov:

After all the horrors I had heard about the 'Moscow Futurists,' I found myself in the company of the most charming people, modest and serious. I recall the degree of admiration with which Larionov described the beauty of Japanese art, with which he was greatly absorbed at the time.

And I recall the thoroughness with which Goncharova discussed each detail of the forthcoming production—how quietly dedicated, sincere, and concentrated she was in all her conversation. Her paintings at first shocked me. In a large dark studio of a gloomy suburban house, we, for some unknown reason, were introduced to her work by candlelight.

The entire room was covered with paintings, all facing the walls. One after another, the canvases were turned around for us to see. At first they frightened me. I did not 'believe' in them. There was a portrait: the face was almost a yard in diameter; I think it had only one eye. I started worrying again about the fate of *Le Coq d'Or*. But gradually I began to acquire a taste for the paintings of this frail, nervous woman.

After a while I began to suspect that her work contained something serious and good. Then I began to appreciate her good taste in colors, and developed an interest in her unusual approach to landscapes.

As soon as we had left Goncharova, I voted in her favor. I never regretted this. Goncharova not only produced marvelous scenery and costume sketches, but also displayed an unbelievably fantastic devotion to work on *Le Coq d'Or*.

It was very touching to observe how she, together with Larionov, painted by hand the entire assortment of stage props. Each object on the stage was a masterpiece.[9]

For the stage sets she painted building façades ornately decorated with primordial flowers, glowing with the effulgent coloration of Eastern art. We are reminded of the animated folk painting which covers the interior walls of such old Byzantine structures as St. Basil's in Moscow.

Larionov was drafted into military service when World War I broke out, but after being wounded and released in 1915 he joined Goncharova, Bakst, and others in the exodus of Russian artists to Switzerland where they joined Diaghilev's "cabinet." The expansive impresario maintained a villa at Ouchy, on the shore of Lake Geneva outside Lausanne. Stravinsky lived conveniently nearby, Ernest Ansermet, the conductor, was within easy distance, and joining the refugee artists in residence at Ouchy was the young dancer Massine. From the brain-trust sessions that followed came the ballet *Liturgy* with scenery and costumes by Goncharova. Her backdrop looked like an iconostasis, similar to that in the Moscow Cathedral of the Assumption, including even the same motif of the pillars covered with images of saints, and the costumes were geometrically conceived—in the emphatic, sharp lines of the Rayonnist style. The Diaghilev entourage made a brief visit to Spain where plans were drafted for ballets with Iberian themes, and then Goncharova and Larionov settled permanently in Paris.

In the post-war years the couple continued to create stage décor for the Ballet Russe. Among Goncharova's highly acclaimed successes were *Les Noces*, for which she designed arrestingly austere sets and costumes, and the spectacular *Firebird*, which revolutionized ballet possibilities through its avant-garde music "painting" by Stravinsky and its synaesthetic color environments realized in Goncharova's contributions (FIGS. 123 and 124). Skilfully she blended the modernism of her stage designs with her Russian heritage. For example, in one setting a series of bulbous cupolas are effectively welded together in an ornamental linear pattern. After Diaghilev's death in 1929, the services of the two artists continued to be in demand by other ballet companies. In the 1930's Goncharova did a new version of *Le Coq d'Or* as well as designing *Cinderella* for Colonel de Basil, and during the next decade she produced sets and costumes for the Ballets du Marquis de Cuevas and for Sadlers' Wells. She even worked as a dress designer but never stopped painting. After the first Sputnik was launched by the Russians in 1957, she began a series of abstract compositions entitled *Space* or *Blue*, suggesting the movement of spheres.

Larionov had a stroke in 1950 which left him slightly paralyzed and unable to work, and in the late fifties Goncharova became crippled with arthritis but still managed to paint. They lived quite frugally in a modest apartment crowded with their work and memorabilia. A visitor recalls climbing five spiral flights and knocking on an impenetrable-looking door. After a pause, some movement and sounds of discussion in Russian were heard. The door opened a little, and he was scrutinized by the calm eyes of Goncharova. He writes, "The interior of the apartment is unique. No walls and almost no ceilings or floors are visible; the three rooms and the little vestibule are crammed from top to bottom with piles of books, parcels of drawings, pictures, portfolios. . . . Gontcharova has the devoted air of a nun. Her grey hair, parted in the middle and dragged back in the humblest way, her anonymous black dress, her folded hands, her silent entries and exits— everything about her conveys an impression of reticence and withdrawal."[10]

The last silent exit of this frail, creative octogenarian was made in 1962. Her husband survived her by two years.

FIG. 119 NATALIA GONCHAROVA, *Spring Gardening*

FIG. 120 NATALIA GONCHAROVA, *Cats*

FIG. 121 NATALIA GONCHAROVA, *Woman in a Hat*, 1912

FIG. 122 NATALIA GONCHAROVA, Costume for the First Prince, *Le Coq d'Or*

FIG. 123 NATALIA GONCHAROVA, Costume for *Firebird*

FIG. 124 SERGE LIFAR, wearing costume designed by Goncharova, 1932

FIG. 125 · NATALIA GONCHAROVA, *Autumn Forest*, 1950

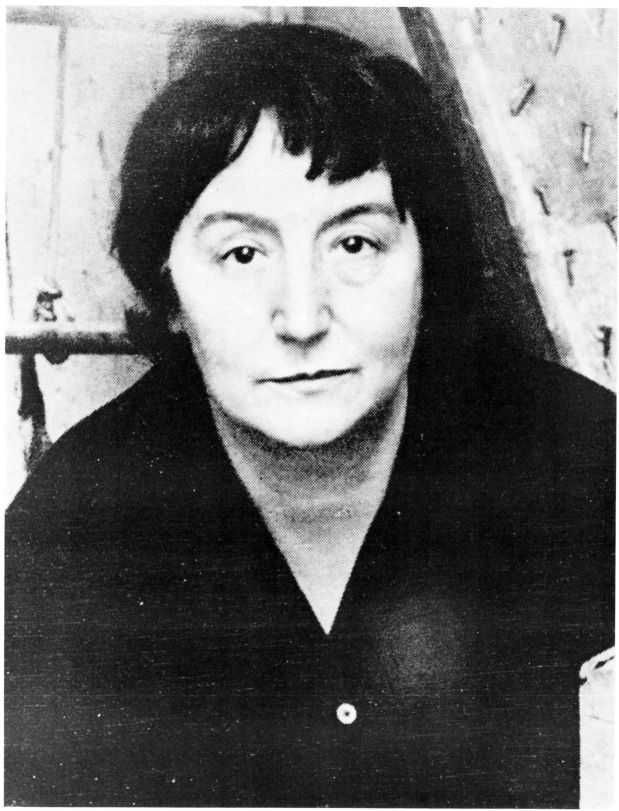

FIG. 126 *Germaine Richier*

GERMAINE RICHIER
1904·1959

THE PRIMORDIAL, stark "hybrids" of Germaine Richier serve as sober testimony to the decaying process of time and stand as twentieth-century totems of anxiety. Archetypal in their evocative power, these lead and bronze monuments, with their agitated surfaces, are a curious blend of human beings with nature—"metamorphoses" as the artist herself refered to them. *Water* (FIG. 133) has a woman's body but in place of a head the handles and neck of an amphora; *Leaf* is a frail, swaying girl whose skin bears the imprint of leaves, and *The Ant* looks undeniably like a seated human being. A knowledge of the circumstances of Richier's early life reveals the sources in nature that were to provide a lifelong stimulus.

Born in September 1904 at the country town of Grans near Arles in southern France, Germaine was the daughter of a vineyard owner who supported a family of four children: two girls and two boys. Early in her childhood the family moved to a farm at Castelnau-le-Nez near Montpellier. As she described the house, it was a dilapidated former monastery with high vaulted cellars, the unchartered territory of which nurtured her love of mystery. The dried-up Lez river nearby also left an important impression on her, for one day this arid trickle suddenly rose to form a river which swept away the family house.[1] Germaine was sent to the Véziat School outside Montpellier, but she greatly disliked the academic discipline and much prefered what the city had to offer in the way of silent, beckoning statues and a magical botanical garden, just as previously she had liked the freedom to wander in the fields of Province. In a rare interview overlooked by the compilers of her bibliography, she is quoted as exclaiming upon this untrammeled aspect of her childhood, "Oh, nature! The animals, the insects! I kept cocoons, in order to watch the silkworms. Oh, the praying mantises, the ants and grasshoppers! I had whole regiments of grasshoppers."[2]

She knew that she wanted to become a sculptor very early, and in Castelnau she began to create numerous figures out of stones and to play with cement,

223

delighting in being able to stop up the challenging holes in walls. The native plane tree, so generously sprinkled over the Midi region of France, also served a formative role. Richier related, "Plane-tree bark forms a kind of tube. That gave me the mold. I poured cement into it. For me, the plane-tree was a tree whose fruit was bark."[3]

Entrance into the École des Beaux-Arts in Montpellier was the eighteen-year-old girl's own decision in 1922. "Oh, my parents were dead set against it! They absolutely detested the notion of a girl's studying at the Beaux-Arts. 'Women aren't made for art,' my father used to say."[4] She studied with Louis-Jacques Guigues, director of the school and a follower of Rodin, and upon completion of the three-year program she managed to quit the South for Paris. The vitalistic sculpture of Antoine Bourdelle, which she had seen at the Marseilles Opera House, convinced her that he should be her teacher. Another young sculptor, Alberto Giacometti, was just completing his study with the master when Richier entered the atelier in 1925. After four years of instruction from Bourdelle she set up her own studio nearby on the Avenue de Maine and began to work independently, doing for the most part uncommissioned portrait busts. Though she sold few, she managed by taking pupils and accepting some help from an encouraging older brother who had become a successful businessman in Marseilles. In 1929 she married a fellow sculptor, the Swiss Otto Bänninger, whom she had met at Bourdelle's atelier, and who had stayed on as the master's assistant.[5]

During the 1930's in Paris Richier witnessed the full flourishing of Surrealism, and she may well have been acquainted with the avant-garde periodical *Minotaure*, which illustrated the works of Dali and the other Surrealist artists. An article on the praying mantis—a typical Surrealist "find" —appeared in the fifth issue of the magazine and must have corroborated her own childhood interest in the motif, for she created several praying mantis representations two decades later.[6] Other new movements were also being initiated—many artists chose to become affiliated with the "Abstraction–Création" group, but Richier's sculpture shows little affinity for these non-objective creations. Instead she continued to assert the human image and to explore new techniques for expression in the medium of bronze.

Official recognition of Richier's work came in 1936 when she received the Blumenthal Prize for Sculpture at the Petit Palais exhibition and the following year the Diploma of Honor at the International Exhibition in Paris. This same year Richier, Suzanne Valadon, Marie Laurencin, and Camille Claudel were among the established artists invited to show in an unusual *Women Artists of Europe* exhibition at the Musée du Jeu de Paume. Twenty-one countries were represented with women's work coming from as far afield as Poland,

Czechoslovakia, Yugoslavia, China, and Japan.

With the outbreak of war in 1939 Richier and Bänninger fled to Switzerland, settling in Bänninger's native city of Zurich. They maintained separate studios, each above the city with a view of the lake.[7] Her work consisted of compelling human figures with animated patinas followed the vigorous style of Bourdelle, whereas his sculpture adhered to a classical tradition. Richier continued to teach. Robert Müller, who studied with her from 1939 to 1944, has become increasingly well-known for his sculpture made of scrap metal. But particularly it was Richier's own example of being a successful woman sculptor which inspired many female students in Switzerland. She founded an "invisible" school of sculptors and was important as an instructor to them.[8]

Many artists lived in Switzerland during the war years. Giacometti was in Geneva, Max Bill was back in Zurich, and, although the Arps had been living in Grasse since 1941, Zurich was the site of an accident which caused the premature death in 1943 of Sophie Täuber-Arp, an outstanding artist of multiple interests. It is likely that Richier was affected by this sudden death of a contemporary.

On her return to liberated France Richier's forms became definitely more brooding and spectral. *Storm*, a massive standing figure, simply looks like a tall man at a distance, but at closer range the viewer sees that the normal facial features are missing and only excrescences and hollows exist. *Rope Dancer*, with its spindly limbs and corroded surface, is another reminder of the holocaust of war and the recent Nazi tyranny. Those favorite insects of Richier's childhood began to appear in magnified semi-human form: a four-foot high *Praying Mantis*, seated on its hind legs, its forelegs dangling menacingly like giant claws, and the *Spider*, enlarged to two feet in height, pitching forward in a frightening lurch. When Richier was asked how a woman from sunny Midi could create such monsters, she replied, "We Southerners look cheerful, but beneath the surface a drama is buried. Arles is a tragic town. When the women go out walking in winter time, with black shawls drawn around their heads to protect them from the cold, they look like macaques [monkeys]."[9]

In the aftermath of the war, major art exhibitions resumed. Richier was included in the 1947 International Exhibition of Surrealism and in the 1948 Biennale in Venice, where she continued to be invited to the subsequent biennales. She was further honored with the sculpture prize at the São Paulo Biennale in 1951, and her works began to find buyers from among the South American museums.

Among her travels of significance was a visit to London in 1947, where she taught sculpture at the Anglo–France Arts Centre and in turn learned the art of engraving.[10] She applied her new technique in illustrations for Rimbaud's *Illuminations* (1951) and for René de Solier's poems *Contre Terre* (1958). Some of the faceless men, spiders, and praying mantises of her sculpture are found in the web-like intricacies of these enigmatic etchings.

Richier's most dramatic sculpture comes from the early 1950's: *Don Quixote of the Forest* (FIG. 128), an over-lifesize figure that is a composite of bronze and dead tree limbs, and *The Devil with Claws* (FIG. 129), whose kneecap is an actual knot of wood and whose lacerated body is matched by a weathered base. The beholder is reminded of Richier's youthful fascination with the bark of the plane trees on the farm at Castelnau. *The Shepherd of the Lands* is a life-size bronze supported disquietly by emaciated legs and surmounted by an eerie skull. In *The Ant* and *The Devil with Claws* tension is heightened by the addition of a criss-cross of tautly drawn wires. *The Minotaur and Siren* (1955) or *Seated Dwarf with Cat's Cradle* (1960) by the Austrian-American Bernard Reder might suggest a contemporary analogy, but his figures are more playful and do not contain the ominous message of Richier's anthropomorphic images. The pathos of her sculpture reflects the *Angst* of post-war Europe, and her creatures are surely more analogous to the seared victims of atomic bombing. As she said, "Our age, when you consider it, is full of talons. People bristle, as they do after long wars. It seems to me that in violent works there is just as much sensibility as in poetic ones. There can be just as much wisdom in violence as in gentleness."[11]

Richier's work has been and may justifiably be characterized as Existential. One sees the acceptance of being, of the inevitability of pain, of the isolation of the individual in her anguished forms. In 1950 when she was commissioned to do a Christ for the church at Assy, she modeled a suffering, attenuated figure, with a flattened body pressed against a simple cross. The overwhelming despair of the image was too mordant for the parishioners, and the crucifix was removed soon after its installation. Only later, after much debate, was it set up again, this time in the mortuary chapel.

During the 1950's Richier experimented with providing her sculptures with environments, a precursor of George Segal's and Edward Kienholz's environmental settings of the 1960's. She arranged with her friend Maria Elena Vieira da Silva that the Portuguese-born artist provide her with a painted background for one of her works, and later Hans Hartung also collaborated with her for a similar joint work. Then Richier began to carve relief sculpture in combination with bronze figurines. She had frequently utilized the whiteness of plaster to portray a *Grasshopper* or a *Praying Mantis* in a semi-disintegrated form. Now in the late 1950's she began to add paint to her plaster sculptures. On other occasions she imbedded broken, colored

226

glass in her lead sculptures, emphasizing the refractive surface but also interiorizing her sculpture as she had earlier with concavities—creating an interpenetration between the surface and the enclosed mass with the result that the exterior shell seemed to invade the underlying form.

When Richier left Zurich, she also separated permanently from her Swiss husband, and in 1955 she married the French writer René de Solier, who has since became an eloquent spokesman for her work. Also, in the mid-1950's Richier was confronted with the shocking news that she had terminal cancer. She returned to her native Province, settling near Arles, and began to do small-scale pieces. Gradually she resumed monumental sculpture, and throughout this time her work continued to be exhibited internationally—in the United States, South America, and Europe (a one-woman show at the Museum of Modern Art in Paris, the Middelheim Biennale in Antwerp, the *Woman as an Artist* exhibition in Zurich, etc.).

In April of 1959 she felt well enough to return to Paris where Alexander Liberman photographed her and wrote, "These are the last photographs of Germaine Richier. She seemed so happy, so full of life and plans. . . . Her studio was clean and luminous; her tools were neatly and precisely arranged. She wore a spotless blue jacket and on it the bright red accent of the Legion of Honor. Kindness radiated around her. She made me want to stay. In her presence one believed in the superior power of love."[12]

A large exhibition of her work was held at the Galerie Creuzevault in Paris, and early in July she visited Antibes on the French Riviera where another exhibition was to open on the 17th at the Musée Grimaldi. Moving on to Montpellier, the ailing Richier died July 31—before reaching her fifty-fifth birthday but while her works, so expressive of the Age of Anxiety, were on public display in Antibes.

FIG. 127 GERMAINE RICHIER, *Portrait*, 1945

FIG. 128 GERMAINE RICHIER, *Don Quixote of the Forest,* 1950–1951

FIG. 131 GERMAINE RICHIER, *Water*, 1953–1954

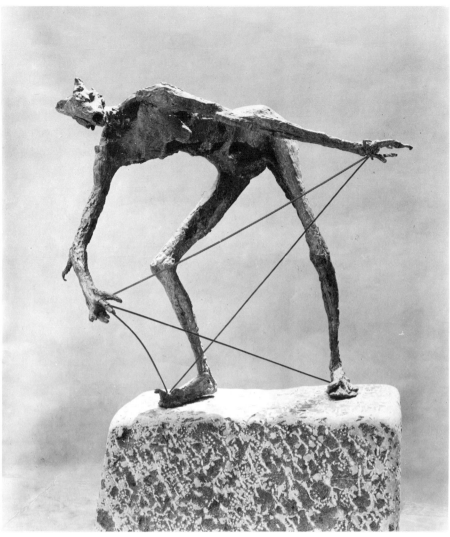

FIG. 129 GERMAINE RICHIER, *The Devil with Claws*, 1952

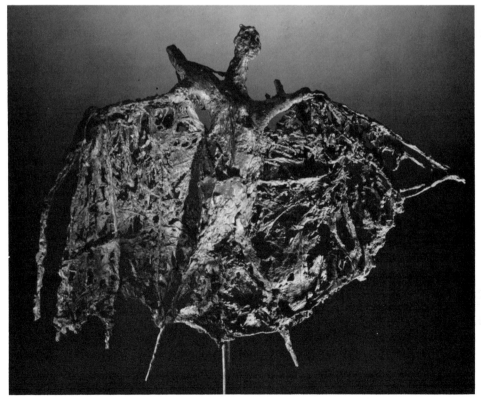

FIG. 130 GERMAINE RICHIER, *The Batman*, 1956

FIG. 132 *I. Rice Pereira*

I. RICE PEREIRA
1907·1971

ACONTEMPORARY of the figurative sculptor Germaine Richier, I. Rice Pereira chose the opposite path in modern art and became, through her public lectures, a crusading spokesman for the abstract. She evolved a distinctive style of geometric abstraction, which she enriched with varying textural treatments, and pioneered with imaginative new materials. Among her innovations was the placing of a sheet of corrugated glass—painted with swatches of transparent color—over her basic composition, thus achieving in her work a suggestion of the time–space concept of modern physics. She was in the vanguard of twentieth-century thinking, attempting to express, both in painting and theoretical writing, the concerns of a cosmological, space-conscious age.

Irene Rice Pereira was born 5 August 1907 in Chelsea, a suburb of Boston, Massachusetts, the eldest child of the German-American Hilda Vanderbilt and her Polish immigrant husband Emanuel Rice. While Irene, fondly called "Gypsy" by her father, was still a small child, her father, of a restless nature himself, moved the family and grain business to western Massachusetts. He settled first in Pittsfield, and then, selling his business there, moved onto Great Barrington, where he bought a bakery. These were happy days for the children as they roamed the Berkshire countryside, discovering the revelations of nature—in particular the reflection of light on dew—but this bucolic freedom was shortlived; when Irene was only eight her father moved the family back to Boston for a year and then to Brooklyn, New York. Six years of permanency followed, but when Irene was fifteen, her father died, and precipitately she found herself in the role of the sole supporter for the family of two younger sisters and a brother. Since her mother was not well and could not help out, the plucky girl switched from the high school's academic courses to its commercial program. She finished three years' work in six months, whereupon she found employment as a stenographer in an accountant's office.

Over the next four years she availed herself of night school classes in clothing design, literature, and art. However, it was the instruction in drawing and painting at Washington Irving High School that captivated her, and she resolved to enter evening classes at the Art Students League in the fall of 1927. Here her principal teachers, the Czech-born Cubist Jan Matulka and the American painter Richard Lahey, introduced Cubism and other modern movements to her, and among her classmates she became friendly with the sculptor David Smith and the painter Burgoyne Diller. Smith, Diller, and Pereira were all to mature into exponents of a rectilinear, abstract style.

In 1929 she married a commercial artist, Humberto Pereira, and by 1931 they felt they had enough money saved to visit Europe. At the last minute she went alone, however, and sailed on the S.S. *Pennland*, making sketches of shipboard details that were later to supply her with thematic inspiration. She enrolled at the Académie Moderne in Paris where the Purist Amédée Ozenfant was a guest professor for the year, but she remained there only a month since the school seemed not to have noticed the modern movements, and the curriculum was based on sketching from life. She traveled to Italy and there discovered with pleasure the golden illumination of Italian Neo-Byzantine paintings. Then, like Klee and Macke before her, she made the voyage to North Africa in search of even purer light, and her first-hand experience of the Sahara Desert was, in her own words, the greatest event in her life.[1] Thereafter, the challenge of conveying infinite space and illumination became an integral aim of her paintings.

Returning to New York in January 1932, I. Rice Pereira devoted her time entirely to painting. The studies of nautical trappings she had made on the ship became the impetus for a whole series of "anchor" canvases which in their imagery suggest a parallel with the contemporary paintings of the American Precisionists Sheeler and Demuth. Her first one-woman exhibition was held in 1933 at the A.C.A. Gallery where at least one critic reviewed the show of "Mr. Pereira's" work.[2]

Her next series of paintings combined machinery with man in a style somewhat analogous to that of the French modernist Leger. In rich colors she painted human figures being dwarfed by machines that they struggled to control. But steadily she progressed toward a non-objective abstraction of the kind fathered by Van Doesburg, the leader of the Dutch De Stijl movement and being developed by the Constructivist painters (such as Moholy-Nagy) at the German Bauhaus.

The Depression caused Pereira to become connected with the WPA's Federal Art Project, and in 1935 she joined the teaching staff of the Design Laboratory, which was modeled on the Bauhaus originally established in

Weimar. The avowed goal of the Laboratory was to stress the inter-relationship of fine arts and design and to encourage experimental work. In particular, it was the textural studies that were to affect Pereira's evolving style.

Retaining only the geometric shapes of her former work, Pereira in 1937 moved into complete abstraction and enriched her canvases by textures obtained through various means such as scraping and incising.[3] She soon observed that pigment freed from representation could produce luminosity and wrote of her work:

> My philosophy is the reality of space and light; an ever-flowing, never-ceasing continuity; unfettered by man-made machinery, weight and external likenesses. I use geometric symbols as they represent structural essences and contain infinite possibilities of change and dynamics.[4]

Two years later, in 1939, she expanded her experiments by doing her first paintings on glass and then eventually on parchment which she found "capable of creating luminosity, as well as retaining relief pattern."[5] Her motivation was to shed old-fashioned modes and to move into a twentieth-century idiom by finding plastic equivalents for the modern advances in mathematics and the sciences.

For a brief time in the early 1940's she pictorially restricted herself to flat, two-dimensional compositions which were severely rectilinear, such as *Three White Squares* (FIG. 133). But within two years she was blending her techniques; we find that in *White Lines* (FIG. 134) the forms remain sharply rectilinear but the surface is enriched by a texture of marble dust and sand. Also at this time museums began to acquire her work beginning with the Newark Museum's purchase of *Composition in White*.

Henceforth in her paintings she sought a deeper space. Using a greater diversity of geometric shapes (frequently including trapezoids) and painting color areas of different transparencies, she achieved the impression of three-dimensional space floating freely forward and backward on her two-dimensional surface. In her treatise *The Nature of Space* she elucidates her intentions:

> . . . we can conclude that this space of the mood—mathematical or philosophical space—is not an abstraction.
> Hence, if this space is no longer an abstraction, we can call this space conceptual space. Conceptual space of the mind is the reality of the space-time continuum. It is the space of creation.[6]

In *Oblique Progression* (FIG. 136) this space–time continuum may be seen; lines and forms overlap and seem to move forward and back in space. The effect is achieved simply with oil: bands and lines of color (pink, yellow, orange) against larger zones of color (blue, brown) which have *trompe l'oeil* textural qualities.

Her invention of superimposing a sheet of corrugated glass over the initial composition increased the vibrant effect of flux in her paintings. For example, the beholder's impression of *Indulating Arrangement* (FIG. 135) changes with his position as he looks through rippled glass at the underlying pattern. The design and depth seem to fluctuate; space glides in and out. Pereira achieves this by applying oil pigments to masonite and then superimposing a second geometric design of lighter pigments on corrugated glass.

Shooting Stars of 1952 (Metropolitan Museum) is composed of three planes. The back is oil on a gesso panel, and the first two are corrugated glass with opaque plastic paint on the middle plane and transparent lacquer on the top. By mounting these layers together, the artist has achieved reflections and refractions of light within the picture itself, creating the impression of continuous movement in space. Her work might be considered the prototype of the neon and fluorescent light constructions of Dan Flavin in the 1960's.

It is interesting to consider the titles of Pereira's paintings, for her choices mirror her change in interests as she developed her philosophical and aesthetic theories. Whereas in the 1940's she gave her paintings geometric names (*Eight Oblongs*, *Transverse Parallels*), in the next decade her titles indicate her cosmic concerns: *Evaporating Night*, *Melting Horizon*, *Sunrise*, *Sunset*, *Incandescent*, *Celestial Gate*. It is as if dazzled by the too-raw confrontation with the sun of the Sahara Desert, Pereira nevertheless retained the intensity of this physical experience and spent the rest of her life translating it into terms the intellect could accept: the direct rays of the sun were deflected into a grid-work diagram of the cosmos. The fervor with which she proselytized half-digested scientific explanations of the universe suggests an inner need for order and direction—qualities sorely lacking in her personal life as, mercurially, she changed husbands three times.

The "gypsy" appellation given to her in childhood seems to have been prophetically descriptive of Pereira's temperament which was, paradoxically, in marked contrast to the "discipline" she imposed upon her art. In 1950, after obtaining her second divorce, she married George Reavey, a poet and teacher. They lived for the ensuing academic year in Manchester, England, which she considered one of the most dismal and lightless places in the world. The experience made Pereira realize the importance to her of light in both her life and work. The next summer Pereira returned to teach at Ball State College in Muncie, Indiana, before her husband joined her in New York that fall.

As many as fifty one-woman exhibitions of Pereira's paintings have been held since the first one in 1933. The largest exhibition of her work was a retrospective at the Whitney Museum in 1953: sixty paintings were shown in a joint-exhibition with the work of another woman painter, Loren MacIver.

In the 1950's Pereira, while continuing to paint, gave literary release to many of her philosophical theories by publishing at her expense several books: *Light and the New Reality*, *The Transformation of 'Nothing' and the Paradox of Space*, *The Nature of Space*, and *The Lapis*. Her writing, including a collection of poems entitled *The Crystal of the Rose*, was dedicated to her sister Dorothy who had died in 1941.

More publications involving teleological questions followed in the next decade: *The Simultaneous Ever-Coming 'To Be,'* *The Finite versus the Infinite*, and *The Transcendental Formal Logic of the Infinite: The Evolution of Cultural Forms*. From the latter, an excerpt relevant to her pictorial concerns, is the following:

> *Geometry is the form of space*; the spatial structure of abstract thought as well as the structural representation of ideas.
>
> The structural dimensionality of space is intuitively conceived according to the law of the propagation of light; and the Formal structure can be objectified from an inner state into an outer one for active visual contemplation.[7]

Pereira's metaphysical musing had great appeal for Oriental thinkers, and in 1968 the Free University of Asia, located in Karachi, awarded her an honorary doctor of philosophy degree, and the Philippine government named her Poet Laureate. From her notebooks and papers on deposit at the Archives of American Art is a letter to Lloyd Goodrich, formerly Director of the Whitney Museum, in which she mentions having had correspondence with universities as disparate as Moscow, Capetown, and Calcutta regarding her books and stating that she had given permission to a Japanese poet to translate *The Nature of Space*.[8]

After four decades of energetic painting activity Pereira's health gave way. She sought the sun and warm climate of the Spanish Costa del Sol and died 11 January 1971 at the resort town of Marbella. Her last few years were spent back in the direct glow of the sun that had so influenced the theme and transformations of her art. One cannot help but think that the bright light rippling on the Mediterranean may have reminded her of her own corrugated, spectrum paintings. Her poem, *The Lake's Dream*, might serve as a fitting epitaph:

The bird of light
and the wind of the sun
meet in the lake's dream.

The still face of the lake's dream
stirred by memories of the past
reflects time passed in its waters.

The earth of springs
marries them in a fountain.
The murmuring union of their love
ripples forever with laughter.[9]

FIG. 133 I. RICE PEREIRA, *Three White Squares*, 1940

FIG. 134 I. RICE PEREIRA, *White Lines*, 1942

FIG. 135 I. RICE PEREIRA, *Undulating Arrangement*, 194

FIG. 136 I. RICE PEREIRA, *Oblique Progression*

NOTES

CHAPTER ONE

1. Bernard Berenson, *Italian Pictures of the Renaissance, Central Italian and North Italian Schools*, Vol. I, London, 1968; Irene Kühnel-Kunze, "Zur Bildniskunst der Sofonisba und Lucia Anguisciola," *Pantheon*, XX (1962); and Marianne Haraszti-Takács, "Nouvelles Données Relatives à la Vie et à l'Oeuvre de Sofonisba Anguissola," *Bulletin du Musée Hongrois des Beaux-Arts*, XXXI (1968).
2. Charles de Tolnay, "Sofonisba Anguissola and her Relations with Michelangelo," *Journal of the Walters Art Gallery*, IV (1941), pp. 116–117.
3. Giorgio Vasari, *The Lives of the Painters, Sculptors, and Architects*, Vol. III, trans. A. B. Hinds, London, 1927, p. 319.
4. In his own way Asdrubale was recognized; according to the seventeenth-century historian Baldinucci, Asdrubale while still a youth was accepted as a member of the city council. (Filippo Baldinucci, *Notizie dei Professori del Disegno*, Vol. 2, Florence, 1846, p. 621.)
5. The identity of this sitter was once suggested to be the Infanta Isabel Clara Eugenia (Friderike Klauner, "Spanische Portraits des 16. Jahrhunderts," *Jahrbuch der Kunsthistorischen Sammlungen in Wien*, LVII [1961], p. 148), but the Infanta's face is broader and longer than her mother's, and on the basis of comparison with the official portraits of these two women in the Prado and elsewhere, I am convinced that this is a likeness of Isabel de Valois.
6. Vasari, *loc cit.*
7 *Ibid.*, p. 320.
8. Maria Kusche, *Juan Pantoja de la Cruz*, Madrid, 1964.
9. Haraszti-Takács, *op. cit.*, pp. 59–67.

CHAPTER TWO

1. Giovanni Battista Baglione, *Le Vite de' Pittori, Scultori, et Architetti*, Rome, 1642, p. 143.
2. Hugh Trevor-Roper, *The Plunder of the Arts*, London, 1970, p. 32.
3. Carlo Cesare Malvasia, *Felsina Pittrice*, Vol. I, Bologna, 1678, and Romeo Galli, *Lavinia Fontana*, Imola, 1940.
4. Galli, *ibid.*, p. 32.
5. Francisco Pachero, *Arte de la Pintura*, Vol. I, 1956, p. 148.

6. F. Francisco de los Santos, *Descripción de San Lorenzo del Escorial*, 1657 and 1698, as quoted in F. J. Sánchez Cantón, *Fuentes literarias para la Historia del Arte Español*, Vol. II, Madrid, 1933. p. 249.
7. Galli, *op. cit.*, pp. 57–73.

CHAPTER THREE

1. She received a salary of £40 a year until her death (Erna Auerbach, *Tudor Artists*, London, 1954, pp. 187–188), £6 higher than Holbein (Ralph Nicholson Wornum, *Life and Works of Hans Holbein*. London, 1867, p. 205). This substantial amount can be appreciated when we know that it was not until many years later, in 1599, that the court miniaturist Nicholas Hilliard, after much cajoling, was finally granted this large a salary (Erna Auerbach, *Nicholas Hilliard*, Boston, 1964, p. 31).
2. While Susanne Horebout was still living in Flanders, Albrecht Dürer bought a painting by her and confided to his diary with astonishment, "It is wonderful that a female should be able to do such a work."
3. M. Risselin-Steenebrugen, "Martine et Catherine Plantin," *Revue Belge d'Archéologie et d'Histoire de l'Art*, XXVI (1957), pp. 169–188.
4. Joseph Destrée, *Les Heures de Notre Dame dites de Hennessy*, Brussels, 1923.
5. Simone Bergmans, "The Miniatures of Levina Teerling," *Burlington Magazine*, LXIV (1934), p. 232.

CHAPTER FOUR

1. Simone Bergmans, "Le problème Jan Van Hemessen, monogrammiste de Brunswick," *Revue Belge d'Archéologie et d'Histoire de l'Art*, XXIII (1955, II), pp. 133–157. Ms. Bergmans believes that the collaborator of the popular genre painter Jan van Hemmessen was his own daughter and that the Monogrammist of Brunswick was Mayken Verhulst. In subsequent articles (in *Revue Belge*, 1958, and in *Bulletin, Musées des Beaux-Arts de Belgigue*, 1965) she continues to point out that, as the pupil of her father, Catharina must have been his collaborator and must be responsible for the small background scenes in her father's otherwise monumental compositions.

CHAPTER FIVE

1. R. Ward Bissell, "Artemisia Gentileschi—A New Documented Chronology," *Art Bulletin*, Vol. L (June 1968), pp. 153–168.
2. Vouet's wife, Virginia da Vezzo, was also a painter. Apparently she had been a student of Vouet's before their marriage in Rome in 1626. They moved to Paris the following year, and she gave drawing lessons to young ladies of well-to-do French families. (William Crelly, *The Painting of Simon Vouet*, New Haven, 1962).
3. Rudolf and Margot Wittkower, *Born Under Saturn*, New York, 1963, pp. 162–163 for translation of documents.
4. Bissell, *op. cit.*, p. 158. Gentileschi may be refering to the wife of Philip IV, Isabel of Bourbon. Works of art were shipped to the king and queen by the Duke of Alcalá, viceroy in Naples from 1629 to 1631.
5. Filippo Baldinucci, *op. cit.*, Vol. 3, and Joachim von Sandrart, *Academie der Bau-, Bild- und Mahlerey-Künste von 1675*, Munich, 1925.

CHAPTER SIX

1. Juliane Harms, "Judith Leyster, Ihr Leben und ihr Werk," *Oud Holland*, Vol. 44 (1927). It is astonishing that no book has been written on this important artist, and it is hoped that archival work will be done to uncover more information on Leyster and that a long-overdue monograph might result.

CHAPTER SEVEN

1. In the fifteenth century the nun Caterina de' Vigri painted altarpieces and was followed in the next century by the highly acclaimed painter Lavinia Fontana and the sculptor Properzia de' Rossi.
2. Luigi Crespi, *Vite de' Pittori Bolognesi*, Rome, 1769.
3. Carlo Cesare Malvasia, *Felsina Pittrice*, Vol. II, Bologna, 1678, p. 574.
4. *Ibid.*, pp. 473–474.
5. *Ibid.*, p. 475.
6. Etching is another one of the arts which daughters of painters seem to have been encouraged to pursue in the Renaissance and Baroque periods, as well as in more recent times. Diana Ghisi in Mantua and Barbara van den Broeck in Antwerp in the sixteenth century precede a plethora of women engravers in the seventeenth century: Teresa del Po who was elected to the Academy of St. Luke in Rome in 1678, Johanna Sybilla Küsel and her two sisters in Augsburg, Susanna Maria von Sandrart in Nuremberg, Magdalena van de Passe in Utrecht, and the Stella sisters in France.
7. Malvasia, *op. cit.*, pp. 479–480. I am indebted to Professor Megan Laird Comini for the translation of this passage.
8. Laura Ragg, *The Women Artists of Bologna*, London, 1907, p. 287.
9. *Mostra Maestri della Pittura del Seicento Emiliano*, Bologna, 1959.

CHAPTER EIGHT

1. This drawing is in the Städelsches Kunstinstitut, Frankfurt am Main.
2. "A Surinam Portfolio," *Natural History*, December 1962, p. 30.
3. The engraving *Of Caterpillars* from this series can be seen at the Museum of Fine Arts in Boston.
4. One of her watercolors for this was recently (1972) used by the Louvre as the poster to announce a Loan Exhibit from the Teyler Museum in Haarlem.
5. "A Surinam Portfolio," *op. cit.*, p. 37.
6. James Duncan, *The Naturalist's Library*, Vol. XL, Edinburgh, 1843, pp. 39–40.
7. Wilfred Blunt (in *The Art of Botanical Illustration*, London, 1950, p. 127) writes, "Maria Sibylla Merian, though primarily an entomologist, was certainly one of the finest botanical artists of the period. . . ."
8. The demand for Merian's work remained unabated, and two years after her death a second edition of her book on the insects of Surinam was printed. Today the rare copies of her works are carefully preserved in such places as the British Museum, Beinecke Library at Yale University, the Bibliothèque Nationale, Paris; the Berlin Museum, the German National Museum in Nuremberg, and the Academy of Science in Leningrad. Dorothea and her husband moved to Leningrad, and this perhaps explains the presence of Maria's Surinam book there.

CHAPTER NINE

1. She may have been inspired in these landscape settings by Aelst's own teacher Otto Marseus van Schrieck (Werner Timm, "Bemerkungen zu einem Stilleben von Rachel Ruysch," *Oud Holland*, LXXVII (1972), pp. 137–138).
2. W. R. Valentiner, "Allegorical Portrait of Rachel Ruysch," *North Carolina Museum of Art Bulletin*, Vol. I (Summer 1957), p. 7.

CHAPTER TEN

1. Roberto Longhi, *Viatico per cinque secoli di pittura venegiana*, Florence, 1946, p. 35. Michael Levey, *Painting in XVIII Century Venice*, London, 1959, pp. 135–146.
2. The Watteau drawing is reproduced in Vittorio Malamani, *Rosalba Carriera*, Bergamo, 1910, p. 55. This monograph also includes Carriera's Parisian diary.

CHAPTER ELEVEN

1. Peter S. Walch, "Angelica Kauffman," unpublished doctoral dissertation, Princeton University, 1969. Walch also notes that Angelica signed herself "Kauffman," so he has maintained this spelling of her name though other books use the standardized form of "Kauffmann."
2. Goethe, *Italian Journey*, trans. by W. H. Auden and Elizabeth Mayer, Baltimore, 1970, p. 472.

244

3. *Ibid.*, p. 363.
4. *Ibid.*, pp. 375–376.

CHAPTER TWELVE

1. *Memoirs of Madame Vigée Lebrun*, trans. by Lionel Strachey, New York, 1907, pp. 27–28.
2. *Ibid.*, p. 49.
3. *Ibid.*, p. 57.
4. W. H. Helm, *Vigée-Lebrun*, Boston, 1915, p. 110.
5. *Memoirs, op. cit.*, p. 72.
6. *Ibid.*, p. 86.
7. Julie Lebrun also became a painter although of little note. (Lada Nikolenko, "The Russian Portraits of Mme Vigée-Lebrun," *Gazette des Beaux-Arts*, 6. Periode, LXX [July–August 1967], p. 118).

CHAPTER THIRTEEN

1. Charles Coleman Sellers, *The Peale Heritage*, Washington County Museum of Fine Arts, Hagerstown, 1963, p. 6.
2. Though Rosalba died just before her second birthday, Rembrandt Peale was later to give the name to a daughter who did live to become a painter.
3. Wilbur H. Hunter, *Miss Sarah Miriam Peale*, The Peale Museum, Baltimore, 1967, p. 6.
4. *Ibid.*, p. 7.
5. *Ibid.*, p. 8.
6. *Idem.*

CHAPTER FOURTEEN

1. Anna Elizabeth Klumpke, *Memoirs of an Artist*, Boston, 1940, p. 81.
2. Charles Sterling and Margaretta Salinger, *French Paintings XIX Century*, Metropolitan Museum, 1966, p. 162.
3. Anna Elizabeth Klumpke, *Rosa Bonheur, Sa Vie, Son Oeuvre*, Paris, 1908, p. 263. The official decree is dated 1865.
4. *Ibid.*, pp. 311–312.

CHAPTER FIFTEEN

1. From an interview with Lewis printed in the *Lorain County News*. Sylvia G. L. Dannett, *Profiles of Negro Womanhood*, Yonkers, 1964, pp. 119–123. A good bibliography on Lewis can be found in William Gerdts, *The White Marmorean Flock*, Vassar College, Poughkeepsie, 1972.
2. Her contemporary Anne Whitney on her return from Rome was given a post teaching sculpture at Wellesley College.
3. John Mercer Langston, *From the Virginia Plantation to the National Capitol*, Hartford, 1894, p. 179.
4. Interview with Lewis during her 1873 visit recorded in the *San Francisco Chronicle*. Philip M. Montesano, "The Mystery of the San Jose Statues," *Urban West*, March/April 1968, p. 25.
5. Margaret Farrand Thorp, *The Literary Sculptors*, Durham, N.C., 1965, p. 79.
6. Louisa Lander from Salem, Massachusetts, became a friend of Hawthorne's and did his portrait bust which is today in Essex Institute, Salem.
7. Van Wyck Brooks, *The Dream of Arcadia*, New York, 1958, p. 173.
8. "Edmonia Lewis," *The Revolution*, VII, No. 16 (20 April 1871). (The editor was Laura Curtis Bullard).
9. Joseph Leach, *Bright Particular Star, The Life and Times of Charlotte Cushman*, New Haven, 1970, p. 335.
10. *Ibid.*, p. 364.
11. "Edmonia Lewis," *loc cit*. One American tourist is quoted as having bought Lewis's marble copy of the Young Augustus, "the best reproduction of the original then offered by any artist in Rome." (L. B. Wyman, *Elizabeth Buffum Chace*, Boston, 1914, pp. 37–38).
12. Montesano, *op. cit.*, p. 26.
13. Mary E. Phillips, *Reminiscences of William Wetmore Story*, New York, 1897, pp. 233–238.
14. Arna Bontemps, *100 Years of Negro Freedom*, New York, 1962, p. 121.
15. "Edmonia Lewis," *loc cit*.

CHAPTER SIXTEEN

1. John Storm, *The Valadon Drama*, New York, 1959, p. 62.
2. *Ibid.*, p. 94.
3. *Ibid.*, p. 259.
4. Florent Fels, *Maurice Utrillo*, Paris, 1930, p. 3.
5. Storm, *op. cit.*, p. 252, and Robert Beachboard, *La Trinité Maudite*, Paris, 1952, p. 180.

CHAPTER SEVENTEEN

1. *The Diary and Letters of Kaethe Kollwitz*, trans. by Richard and Clara Winston, Chicago, 1955, p. 62.
2. *Ibid.*, p. 122.
3. *Ibid.*, p. 74.
4. *Ibid.*, p. 89.
5. *Ibid.*, p. 104.
6. Otto Nagel, *Käthe Kollwitz*, Greenwich, Conn., 1971, p. 78.
7. *Ibid.*, p. 75.
8. *The Diary and Letters of Kaethe Kollwitz, op. cit.*, p. 198.
9. *Ibid.*, p. 96.
10. *Ibid.*, p. 199.

CHAPTER EIGHTEEN

1. Nora Wydenbruck, *Rilke, Man and Poet*, London, 1949, p. 68.
2. Eliza Marian Butler, *Rainer Maria Rilke*, Cambridge, England, 1961, p. 100, quoting Rilke's diary.
3. Paula Modersohn-Becker, *Briefe und Tagebuchblätter*, Berlin, 1920, pp. 122–123. A translation of this book into English is long overdue.
4. *Ibid.*, pp. 249–250.
5. Rainer Maria Rilke, *Worpswede*, Leipzig, 1903.
6. Modersohn-Becker, *op. cit.*, pp. 61–62. I am grateful to Professor Marga Brockhagen for translating this poem for me.

CHAPTER NINETEEN

1. Augustus John, "Gwendolen John," *Burlington Magazine*, LXXXI (1942), p. 238.
2. Mary Taubman, *Gwen John*, The Arts Council, London, 1968, p. 7.
3. Augustus John, *Chiaroscuro*, New York, 1952, pp. 12–13.
4. Augustus writes about rummaging through dusty books in the attic and finding among other treasures *Jane Eyre* by Currer Bell. He makes no mention of Charlotte Brontë's having submited her novel to the publisher under this pseudonym, but it is a reminder to us of the problems faced by an aspiring woman author a hundred years ago. Gwen John's own life even has echoes of Charlotte Brontë's years of sparse living on the Continent. (Winifred Gérin, *Charlotte Brontë*, Oxford, 1967).
5. John, *Chiaroscuro, op. cit.*, pp. 247–248.
6. *Ibid.*, p. 49.
7. *Ibid.*, p. 66.
8. *Gwen John*, Arts Council catalog with introduction by Augustus John, London, 1946, p. 2.
9. John Rothenstein, *Modern English Painters: Sickert to Smith*, London, 1952, pp. 166–167.
10. *Ibid.*, p. 169.
11. *Ibid.*, p. 172.
12. John, *Chiaroscuro, op. cit.*, pp. 254–255.
13. In 1944 Augustus John was runner-up for the office of President of the Royal Academy. In this election the painter Dame Laura Knight received one vote for the position. (Sidney C. Hutchison, *The History of the Royal Academy 1768–1968*, New York, 1968, p. 182). It should be noted that after the inclusion of two women as founders of the Royal Academy in 1768, no women were admitted until Annie Swynnerton was made an Associate in 1922 and Laura Knight a full member in 1936.

CHAPTER TWENTY

1. Mary Chamot and Camilla Gray, *A Retrospective Exhibition of Paintings and Designs for the Theatre: Larionov and Goncharova*, London, 1961, (p. 46).
2. Camilla Gray, "The Russian Contribution to Modern Painting," *Burlington Magazine*, CII (1960), p. 206.
3. *Ibid.*, p. 209.
4. Camilla Gray, *The Great Experiment: Russian Art 1863–1922*, New York, 1962, p. 142. Other Russian women artists who are mentioned in this book are Alexandra Exter, Elena Polenova, Liubov Popova, Olga Rosanova, Varvara Stepanova, Nadezhda Udaltsova, and Maria Yakunchikova.
5. Chamot in *A Retrospective . . . , op. cit.*, cat. no. 108, believes that this may be Goncharova's first Rayonnist painting and proposes a date of 1911, but Angelica Rudenstine in the forthcoming *The Solomon R. Guggenheim Museum: Paintings, 1880–1945* suggests that *Cats* was probably painted in 1913.
6. Mary Chamot, "The Early Work of Goncharova and Larionov," *Burlington Magazine*, XCVII (1955), p. 173. For fuller discussion see Mary Chamot's new book, *Gontcharova*, Paris, 1972.

7. Igor Stravinsky and Robert Craft, *Conversations with Igor Stravinsky*, New York, 1959, p. 111.
8. Gray, *The Great Experiment, op. cit.*, p. 128.
9. Michel Fokine, *Memoirs of a Ballet Master*, Boston, 1961, pp. 227–228.
10. Richard Buckle, *In Search of Diaghilev*, London, 1955, p. 72.

CHAPTER TWENTY-ONE

1. Paul Guth, "Encounter with Germaine Richier," *Yale French Studies*, Vol. 19–20 (Spring 1957–Winter 1958), p. 79. This important interview supplies many vital facts that have for some reason not been recorded about Richier in any of the literature, not even by her husband.
2. *Idem.*
3. *Ibid.*, p. 80.
4. *Idem.*
5. Heinrich Rumpel, "Otto Charles Bänninger," *Werk*, Vol. 37 (1950), pp. 194 ff.
6. A recent article by William Pressly in the *Art Bulletin*, Vol. LV (December 1973), on the subject of "The Praying Mantis in Surrealist Art," despite references to many "praying mantis" artists in both text and footnotes, characteristically overlooks the woman artist, Germaine Richier, perhaps the most impressive "praying mantis" creator of them all.
7. Nesto Jacometti, "Germaine Richier," *Vie, Art, Cité*, Vol. 3 (1946), p. 28.
8. "Germaine Richier," *Werk*, Vol. 50 (1963), (n.p.).
9. Guth, *op. cit.*, p. 83. It is interesting to observe that when the English artist Graham Sutherland visited the Midi in 1952, he too began to paint grasshoppers and mantises.
10. *Germaine Richier*, Arts Club of Chicago, 1966 (Introduction by René de Solier).
11. Guth, *op. cit.*, p. 82.
12. Alexander Liberman, *The Artist in his Studio*, New York, 1960, p. 282.

CHAPTER TWENTY-TWO

1. John I. H. Baur, *Loren MacIver, I. Rice Pereira*, Whitney Museum of American Art, New York, 1953, p. 45. Baur gives a useful, full account of Pereira's life and stylistic development.
2. *Ibid.*, p. 47.
3. *Ibid.*, p. 51.
4. *American Painting Today* (edited by Nathaniel Pousette-Dart), New York, 1956, p. 42.
5. *Fourteen Americans*, Museum of Modern Art, New York, 1946, p. 44 (her own statement).
6. I. Rice Pereira, *The Nature of Space*, New York, 1956, p. 62.
7. I. Rice Pereira, *The Transcendental Formal Logic of the Infinite: The Evolution of Cultural Forms*, New York, 1966, p. 58.
8. I. Rice Pereira, Roll D222, Archives of American Art, New York.
9. I. Rice Pereira, *The Crystal of the Rose*, New York, 1959, p. 52.

BIBLIOGRAPHY

"A Surinam Portfolio," *Natural History*, December 1962, pp. 28–41

A World of Flowers, Philadelphia Museum of Art, Philadelphia, 1963

Acton, Harold, *The Bourbons of Naples*, London, 1956

Adair, Virginia and Lee, *Eighteenth Century Pastel Portraits*, London, 1971

Adriani, Gert, *Anton Van Dyck Italienisches Skizzenbuch*, Vienna, 1940

The Age of Neo-Classicism, Arts Council of Great Britain, London, 1972

Amberg, George, *Art in Modern Ballet*, New York, 1946

American Masters, 18th and 19th Centuries, Kennedy Galleries, New York, 1972

American Painting Today (ed. Nathaniel Pousette-Dart), New York, 1956

Auerbach, Erna, *Nicholas Hilliard*, Boston, 1964

—, *Tudor Artists*, London, 1954

Baglione, Giovanni Battista, *Le Vite de' Pittori, Scultori, et Architetti*, Rome, 1642

Baldinucci, Filippo, *Notizie dei Professori del Disegno* Florence, 1846

Baur, John I. H., *Loren MacIver, I. Rice Pereira*, Whitney Museum of American Art, New York, 1953

Beachboard, Robert, *La Trinité Maudite*, Paris, 1952

Berenson, Bernard, *Italian Pictures of the Renaissance, Central Italian and North Italian Schools*, London, 1968

Bergmans, Simone, "The Miniatures of Levina Teerling," *Burlington Magazine*, LXIV (1934), pp. 232–236

—, "Note complémentaire à l'étude des De Hemessen, de van Amstel et du monogrammiste de Brunswick," *Revue Belge d'Archéologie et l'Histoire de l'Art*, XXVII (1958), pp. 77–83

—, "Le problème du Monogrammiste de Brunswick," *Bulletin, Musées Royaux des Beaux-Arts de Belgique*, XIV (1965), pp. 143–162

—, "Le problème Jan Van Hemessen, monogrammiste de Brunswick," *Revue Belge d'Archéologie et d'Histoire de l'Art*, XXIII (1955, II), pp. 133–157

Bergström, Ingvar, *Dutch Still-Life Painting in the Seventeenth Century*, New York, 1956

Bernt, Walther, *Netherlandish Painters of the 17th Century*, II, London, 1970

Bissell, R. Ward, "Artemisia Gentileschi—A New Documented Chronology," *Art Bulletin*, L (1968), pp. 153–168

Blunt, Wilfred, *The Art of Botanical Illustration*, London, 1950

Bonetti, Carlo, "Nel centario di Sofonisba Anguissola," *Archivo Storico Lombardo*, LV (1928), pp. 285–306

Bontemps, Arna, *100 Years of Negro Freedom*, New York, 1962

Bowness, Alan, *Modern Sculpture*, London, 1965

Brooks, Van Wyck, *The Dream of Arcadia*, New York, 1958

Buckle, Richard, *In Search of Diaghilev*, London, 1955

Burr, James, "Toad, Bat, Spider, or Man," *Apollo*, XCVII (1973), pp. 53–54

Busiri Vici, Andrea, "Angelica Kauffmann and the Bariatinskis," *Apollo*, LXXVII (1963), pp. 201–208

Butler, Eliza Marian, *Rainer Maria Rilke*, Cambridge, England, 1961

Bunoust, Madeleine, *Quelques femmes peintres*, Paris, 1936

Caravaggio e Caravaggeschi nelle Gallerie di Firenze, Florence, 1970

Carriera, Rosalba, *Journal*, trans. by Alfred Sensier, Paris, 1865

Cassou, Jean, *Germaine Richier*, New York, 1961

Cent dessins du Musée Teyler, Haarlem, Musée du Louvre, Paris, 1972

Chamberlain, Arthur B., *Hans Holbein*, New York, 1913

Chamot, Mary, "The Early Work of Goncharova and Larionov," *Burlington Magazine*, XCVII (1955), pp. 170–174

—, *Gontcharova*, Paris, 1972

—, "Russian 'Avant-garde' Graphics," *Apollo*, XCVIII (1973), pp. 494–501

Chamot, Mary and Camilla Gray, *A Retrospective Exhibition of Paintings and Designs for the Theatre; Larionov and Goncharova*, London, 1961

Clayton, Ellen C., *English Female Artists*, London, 1876

Clement, Clara E., *Women in the Fine Arts*, Boston, 1904

Colding, Torben H., *Aspects of Miniature Painting*, Copenhagen, 1953

Cook, Herbert, "More Portraits by Sofonisba Anguissola," *Burlington Magazine*, XXVI (1915), pp. 228–236

Crelly, William, *The Painting of Simon Vouet*, New Haven, 1962

247

Craven, Wayne, *Sculpture in America*, New York, 1968

Crespi, Luigi, *La Certosa di Bologna*, Bologna, 1772

—, *Vite de' Pittori Bolognesi*, Rome, 1769

Dannett, Sylvia G. L., *Profiles of Negro Womanhood*, Yonkers, 1964

Davies, Martin, *French School*, National Gallery, London, 1970

Destrée, Joseph, *Les Heures de Notre Dame dites de Hennessy*, Brussels, 1923

Deutsch, O. E., "Sir William Hamilton's Picture Gallery," *Burlington Magazine*, LXXXII (1943), pp. 36–41

Donati, Ugo, *Artisti Ticinesi a Roma*, Bellinzona, 1942

Dover, Cedric, *American Negro Art*, Greenwich, 1960

Dürer, Albrecht, *Tagebücher und Briefe*, Munich, 1927

Duncan, James, *The Naturalist's Library*, XL, Edinburgh, 1843

Dutch Masterpieces from the Eighteenth Century, Minneapolis Art Institute, Minneapolis, 1971

Ellet, Elizabeth Fries, *Women Artists in All Ages and Countries*, New York, 1859

Edwards, Evelyn Foster, "Elisabetta Sirani," *Art in America*, XVII (1928–1929), pp. 242–246

Emiliani, Andrea, *La Pinacoteca Nazionale di Bologna*, Bologna, 1967

European Masters of the Eighteenth Century, Royal Academy, London, 1954

Fels, Florent, *Maurice Utrillo*, Paris, 1930

Les Femmes Artistes d'Europe, Musée du Jeu de Paume, Paris, 1937

Fokine, Michel, *Memoirs of a Ballet Master*, Boston, 1961

Foster, Joshua J., *British Miniature Painters and their Works*, London, 1898

Fourteen Americans, Museum of Modern Art, New York, 1946

From Realism to Symbolism, Whistler and his World, New York, 1971

From Ricci to Tiepolo, Palazzo Ducale, Venice, 1969

Furst, Herbert, *The Art of Still Life Painting*, London, 1927

Galli, Romeo, *Lavinia Fontana*, Imola, 1940

Gerdts, William, *American Neo-Classical Sculpture*, New York, 1973

—, *The White Marmorean Flock*, Vassar College, Poughkeepsie, 1972

Gérin, Winifred, *Charlotte Brontë*, Oxford, 1967

Giedion-Welcker, Carola, *Contemporary Sculpture*, New York, 1960

Gontcharova/Larionov, Musée d'Art Moderne de la Ville de Paris, Paris, 1963

Gonzalez-Palacios, Alvar, "Le Pavillon de Flore," *The Connoisseur*, CLXXIV (1970), pp. 188–190

Grant, Maurice H., *Rachel Ruysch, 1664–1750*, Leigh-on-Sea, 1956

Gray, Camilla, *The Great Experiment: Russian Art 1863–1922*, New York, 1962

—, "The Russian Contribution to Modern Painting," *Burlington Magazine*, CII (1960), pp. 205–211

Grigoriev, Sergio L., *The Diaghilev Ballet 1909–1929*, London, 1953

Guicciardini, Ludovico, *Description de tout le Pays-Bas*, Antwerp, 1567

Guilleminault, Gilbert, *Les Maudits de Cézanne à Utrillo*, Paris, 1959, for Anne Manson, "Suzanne Valadon la Frénétique," pp. 249–311

Guth, Paul, "Encounter with Germaine Richier," *Yale French Studies*, XIX–XX (1957–1958), pp. 78–84

Goethe, Johann Wolfgang, *Italian Journey*, trans. by W. H. Auden & Elizabeth Mayer, Baltimore, 1970

Hammacher, Abraham Marie, *The Evolution of Modern Sculpture*, New York, 1969

Hanaford, Phebe A., *Daughters of America*, Augusta, Maine, 1883

Haraszti-Takács, Marianne, "Nouvelles Données Relatives à la Vie et à l'Oeuvre de Sofonisba Anguissola," *Bulletin du Musée Hongrois des Beaux-Arts*, XXXI (1968), pp. 53–67

Harms, Juliane, "Judith Leyster, Ihr Leben und ihr Werk," *Oud Holland*, XLIV (1927), pp. 88–96, 112–126, 145–154, 221–242, 275–279

Hartcup, Adeline, *Angelica*, London, 1954

Haskell, Arnold L., *Diaghileff*, New York, 1935

Helm, William Henry, *Vigée-Lebrun*, Boston, 1915

Hildebrandt, Hans, *Die frau als künstlerin*, Berlin, 1928

Hill, George Francis, *Portrait Medals of Italian Artists of the Renaissance*, London, 1912

Hitchcock, Henry-Russell, *Painting toward Architecture*, New York, 1948

Hofstede de Groot, Cornelis, "Schilderijen door Judith Leyster," *Oud Holland*, XLVI (1929), pp. 25–26

Holmes, C. J., "S. Anguissola and Philip II," *Burlington Magazine*, XXVI (1915), pp. 181–187

Hunter, Wilbur H., *Miss Sarah Miriam Peale*, The Peale Museum, Baltimore, 1967

Hutchison, Sidney C., *The History of the Royal Academy 1768–1968*, New York, 1968

Illustrated Catalogue of Early English Portraiture, Burlington Fine Arts Club, London, 1909

Jacometti, Nesto, "Germaine Richier," *Vie, Art, Cité*, III (1946), (p. 28)

—, *Suzanne Valadon*, Geneva, 1947

John, Augustus, *Chiaroscuro*, New York, 1952

—, "Gwendolen John," *Burlington Magazine*, LXXXI (1942), pp. 237–238

Gwen John, The Arts Council of Great Britain, London, 1946

Angelika Kauffmann und ihre Zeitgenossen, Bregenz, 1968

Keppler, Uta, *Die Falterfrau*, Heibronn, 1963

Klauner, Friderike, "Spanische Portraits des 16. Jahrhunderts," *Jahrbuch des Kunsthistorischen Sammlungen in Wien*, LVII (1961), pp. 123–158

Klumpke, Anna Elizabeth, *Memoirs of an Artist*, Boston, 1940

—, *Rosa Bonheur, Sa Vie, Son Oeuvre*, Paris, 1908

Kochno, Boris, *Diaghilev and the Ballets Russes*, trans., New York, 1970

Kollwitz, Käthe, *The Diary and Letters*, trans. by Richard and Clara Winston, Chicago, 1955

Kühnel-Kunze, Irene, "Zur Bildniskunst der Sofonisba und Lucia Anguisciola, *Pantheon*, XX (1962), pp. 83–96

Kusche, Maria, *Juan Pantoja de la Cruz*, Madrid, 1964

Langston, John Mercer, *From the Virginia Plantation to the National Capitol*, Hartford, 1894

Larkin, Oliver, W., *Art and Life in America*, New York,

1949

Leach, Joseph, *Bright Particular Star, The Life and Times of Charlotte Cushman*, New Haven, 1970

Lebel, Robert, "L'Irruption des Femmes dans la Sculpture," *XX Siècle*, XXX (1968), pp. 131–140

Lendorff, Gertrude, *Maria Sibylla Merian 1647–1717, Ihr Leben und ihr Werk*, Basle, 1955

Levey, Michael, "Notes on the Royal Collection—II, Artemisia Gentileschi's 'Self-Portrait' at Hampton Court," *Burlington Magazine*, CIV (1962), pp. 79–80

—, *Painting in XVIII Century Venice*, London, 1959

"Edmonia Lewis," *The Negro History Bulletin*, II (1939), p. 51

"Edmonia Lewis," *The Revolution*, VII, No. 16 (20 April 1871)

Liberman, Alexander, *The Artist in his Studio*, New York, 1960

The Serge Lifar Collection of Ballet Set and Costume Designs, Wadsworth Atheneum, Hartford, 1965

Litta, Pompeo, *Famiglie Celebri Italiane*, V, Milan, 1839

Loguine, Tatiana, *Gontcharova et Larionov*, Paris, 1971

Long, Basil S., *British Miniaturists*, London, 1929

Longhi, Roberto, *Viatico per cinque secoli di pittura venegiana*, Florence, 1946

Lynes, Russell, *The Art-Makers of Nineteenth-Century America*, New York, 1970

MacLaren, Neil, *The Dutch School*, National Gallery, London, 1960

Madsen, Karl, *Fortegnelse over Malerisamlingen pa Nivaagaard*, Copenhagen, 1949

Les Maîtres de l'art indépendant 1895–1937, Petit Palais, Paris, 1937

Malamani, Vittorio, *Rosalba Carriera*, Bergamo, 1910

Malvasia, Carlo Cesare, *Felsina Pittrice*, Bologna, 1678

Manaresi, Antonio, *Elisabetta Sirani*, Bologna, 1898

Mancini, Giulio, *Viaggio di Roma per Vedere le Pitture*, Leipzig, 1923

Mander, Carel van, *Le Livre des Peintres*, Paris, 1884

Manners, Lady Victoria and G. C. Williamson, *Angelica Kauffmann, R.A., Her Life and Works*, London, 1924

Mathey, François, *Six Femmes Peintres*, Paris, 1951

Mauceri, Enrico, "Nella Pittura Bolognese Lavinia Fontana, *Revista Mensile del Comune*, July–August 1936, pp. 15–17

Mayer, Dorothy Moulton, *Angelica Kauffmann, R.A., 1741–1807*, Gerrards Cross, 1972

Mercer, Eric, *English Art 1553–1625*, Oxford, 1962

Minghetti, Marco, "Le donne italiane nelle Belle Arti al secolo XV e XVI," *Nuova Antologia*, XXXV (1877), pp. 308–330

Modersohn-Becker, Paula, *Briefe und Tagebuchblätter*, Berlin, 1920

Moir, Alfred, *The Italian Followers of Caravaggio*, Cambridge, Mass., 1967

Montesano, Philip M., "The Mystery of the San Jose Statues," *Urban West*, March/April 1968, pp. 25–27

La Mostra della Pittura Napoletana dei Secoli XVII, XVIII, XIX, Naples, 1938

Mostra Maestri della Pittura del Seicento Emiliano, Bologna, 1959

Myers, Bernard, *The German Expressionists*, New York, 1963

Nagel, Otto, *Käthe Kollwitz*, Greenwich, 1971

Neilson, Winthrop and Frances, *Seven Women: Great Painters*, Philadelphia, 1969

Neurdenburg, Elisabeth, "Judith Leyster," *Oud Holland*, XLVI (1929), pp. 27–30

The New Decade, Museum of Modern Art, New York, 1955

Nichols, John Gough, "Notices of the Contemporaries and Successors of Holbein," *Archaelogia*, XXX (1863), pp. 39–40

Nicolson, Benedict, "Caravaggesques in Florence," *Burlington Magazine*, CXII (1970), pp. 636–641

Nikolenko, Lada, "The Russian Portraits of Mme Vigée-Lebrun," *Gazette des Beaux-Arts*, 6.Periode, LXX (1967), pp. 91–120

Nochlin, Linda, "Why Have There Been No Great Women Artists," *Art News*, LXIX (1971), pp. 22–39, 67–71

Ojetti, Ugo, L. Dami and N. Tarchiani, *La pittura italiana del seicento e del settecento alla Mostra di Palazzo Pitti*, Milan and Rome, 1924

Orbaan, J. A. F., *Documenti sul barocco in Roma*, Rome, 1920

Osten, Gert von der and Horst Vey, *Painting and Sculpture in Germany and The Netherlands: 1500–1600*, Baltimore, 1969

Oulmont, Charles, *Les Femmes Peintres du Dix-Huitième Siècle*, Paris, 1928

Pacheco, Francisco, *Arte de la Pintura*, Madrid, 1956

The Peale Family, Detroit, 1967

Pepper, D. Stephen, "Guido Reni's 'Il Diamante': A New Masterpiece for Toledo," *Burlington Magazine*, CXV (1973), p. 635

Pereira, I. Rice, *The Crystal of the Rose*, New York, 1959

—, *The Finite versus the Infinite*, New York, 1962

—, *The Lapis*, New York, 1957

—, Letter to the Editor, *Art Voices*, IV, No. 2 (1965), p. 80

—, *Light and the New Reality*, New York, 1951

—, Roll D222, Archives of American Art, New York

—, Roll D223, Archives of American Art, New York

—, *The Simultaneous Ever-Coming 'To Be,'* New York, 1961

—, *The Transcendental Formal Logic of the Infinite: The Evolution of Cultural Forms*, New York, 1966

—, *The Transformation of 'Nothing' and the Paradox of Space*, New York, 1953

I. Rice Pereira, Amel Gallery, New York, 1962

I. Rice Pereira, Galerie Internationale, New York, 1964

Pérez Sánchez, Alfonso E., *Pintura italiana del siglo XVII en España*, Madrid, 1965

Pevsner, Nikolaus, *Academies of Art*, Cambridge, England, 1940

Phillips, Mary E., *Reminiscences of William Wetmore Story*, New York, 1897

Pignatti, Terisio, *Il Museo Correr di Venezia, Dipinto del XVII e XVIII secolo*, Venice, 1960

Placenta, Raymond, *School of Paris*, Greenwich, 1960

Porter, James A., *Modern Negro Art*, New York, 1943

Pressly, William, "The Praying Mantis in Surrealist Art," *Art Bulletin*, LV (1973), pp. 600–615

Ragg, Laura, *The Women Artists of Bologna*, London, 1907

Rathbone, Perry, *The Forsyth Wickes Collection*, Museum of Fine Arts, Boston, 1968

Renraw, R., "The Art of Rachel Ruysch," *Connoisseur*, XCII (1933), pp. 397–399

Rewald, John, *Post-Impressionism*, New York, 1956

Reynolds, Graham, *Connoisseur Period Guides, Tudor*, New York, 1956

Germaine Richier, Arts Club of Chicago, Chicago, 1966 (Introduction by René de Solier)

Germaine Richier, Hannover Gallery, London, 1955 (Introduction by David Sylvester)

Germaine Richier, Martha Jackson Gallery, New York, 1957 (Introduction by René de Solier)

Germaine Richier, Musée National d'Art Moderne, Paris, 1956

"Germaine Richier," *Werk*, L (1963), (n.p.)

Germaine Richier 1904–1959, Galerie Creuzevault, Paris, 1966

Rilke, Rainer Maria, *Requiem and Other Poems*, trans. by J. B. Leishman, London, 1935

—, *Worpswede*, Leipzig, 1903

Rischbieter, Henning, *Art and the Stage in the Twentieth Century*, Greenwich, 1972

Risselin-Steenebrugen, M., "Martine et Catherine Plantin," *Revue Belge d'Archéologie et l'Histoire de l'Art*, XXVI (1957), pp. 169–188

Roblot-Delondre, Louise, *Portraits d'Infantes XVIe Siècle*, Paris and Brussels, 1913

Rodocanachi, Emmanuel, *La Femme italienne avant, pendant et après la renaissance*, Paris, 1922

Rothenstein, John, *Modern English Painters: Sickert to Smith*, London, 1952

Rudenstine, Angelica, "The Chronology of Larionov's Early Work," *Burlington Magazine*, CXIV (1972), p. 874

Rücker, Elizabeth, *Maria Sibylla Merian*, Germanisches Nationalmuseum, Nürnberg, 1967

Rumpel, Heinrich, "Otto Charles Bänninger," *Werk*, XXXVII (1950), pp. 149–156

Sachs, Hannelore, *The Renaissance Woman*, New York, 1971

Sánchez Cantón, Francisco J., *Archivo Documental Español*, X, Madrid, 1956–1959

—, *Fuentes literarias para la Historia del Arte Español*, Madrid, 1933

Sandrart, Joachim von, *Academie der Bau-, Bild- und Mahlerey-Künste von 1675*, Munich, 1925

Schlocker, Georges, "Zum Tode Germaine Richiers," *Kunstwerk*, XIII (1959–1960), p. 65

Schneider, Arthur von, *Caravaggio und die Niederländer*, Amsterdam, 1967

Sellers, Charles Coleman, *Charles Willson Peale*, New York, 1969

—, *The Peale Heritage*, Washington County Museum of Fine Arts, Hagerstown, 1963

Selz, Peter, *German Expressionist Painting*, Berkeley, 1957

—, *New Images of Man*, Museum of Modern Art, New York, 1959

Seuphor, Michel, *Sculpture of this Century*, New York, 1960

Le Siècle de Bruegel, Brussels, 1963

Slatkes, Leonard, "The Age of Rembrandt," *Art Quarterly*, XXXI (1968), p. 88

Slive, Seymour, *Frans Hals*, London, 1970

Soby, James Thrall, *Contemporary Painters*, New York, 1948

Solier, René de, "Germaine Richier," *Cahiers d'Art*, XXVIII (1953), Part I, pp. 123–129

Sparrow, Walter Shaw, *Women Painters of the World*, New York, 1905

Spear, Richard, *Caravaggio and His Followers*, Cleveland Museum of Art, Cleveland, 1971

—, "Caravaggisti at the Palazzo Pitti," *Art Quarterly*, XXXIV (1971), p. 110

Stanton, Theodore, *Reminiscences of Rosa Bonheur*, London, 1910

Stechow, Wolfgang, *Catalogue of European and American Paintings and Sculpture*, Allen Memorial Art Museum, Oberlin College, Oberlin, 1967

Stelzer, Otto, *Paula Modersohn-Becker*, Berlin, 1958

Sterling, Charles, *A Catalogue of French Paintings XV–XVIII Centuries*, Metropolitan Museum, New York, 1955

Sterling, Charles and Margaretta Salinger, *French Paintings XIX Century*, Metropolitan Museum, New York, 1966

Stirling-Maxwell, William, *Annals of the Artists of Spain*, London, 1891

Storm, John, *The Valadon Drama*, New York, 1959

Strachan, W. J., "Sculptors as book-illustrators," *The Connoisseur*, CLXXIII (1970), p. 156

Stravinsky, Igor and Robert Craft, *Conversions with Igor Stravinsky*, New York, 1959

Strong, Roy C., *Portraits of Queen Elizabeth I*, Oxford, 1963

Stuldreher-Nienhuis, J., *Verborgen paradijzen; het leven en de werken van Maria S. Merian, 1647–1717*, Arnhem, 1945

Taft, Lorado, *History of American Sculpture*, New York, 1930

Taubman, Mary, *Gwen John*, The Arts Council, London, 1968

Thorp, Margaret Farrand, *The Literary Sculptors*, Durham, N.C., 1965

Timm, Werner, "Bemerkungen zu einem Stilleben von Rachel Ruysch," *Oud Holland*, LXXVII (1972), pp. 137–138

Tolnay, Charles de, "Sofonisba Anguissola and her Relations with Michelangelo," *Journal of the Walters Art Gallery*, IV (1941), pp. 115–119

Tomory, Peter A., "Angelica Kauffmann—'Sappho,'" *Burlington Magazine*, CXIII (1971), pp. 275–276

Trevor-Roper, Hugh, *The Plunder of the Arts*, London, 1970

Tufts, Eleanor, "Sofonisba Anguissola, Renaissance Woman," *Art News*, LXXI (1972), pp. 50–53

—, "Ms. Lavinia Fontana from Bologna: A Successful 16th-Century Portraitist," *Art News*, LXXIII (1974), pp. 60–64

Suzanne Valadon, Musée National d'Art Moderne, Paris, 1967

Valentiner, Wilhelm R., "Allegorical Portrait of Rachel Ruysch," *North Carolina Museum of Art Bulletin*, I (1957), pp. 5–8

Vasari, Giorgio, *The Lives of the Painters, Sculptors, and Architects*, London, 1927

Venturi, Adolfo, *Storia dell'arte italiana,* IX, Parte VI. Milan, 1933

Vigée-LeBrun, Elisabeth, *Memoirs,* trans. by Lionel Strachey, New York, 1907

Waagen, Gustav, *Galleries and Cabinets of Art in Great Britain,* London, 1857

—, *Treasures of Art in Great Britain,* London, 1854

Walch, Peter S., "Angelica Kauffmann and her Contemporaries," *Art Bulletin,* LI (1969), pp. 83–85

—, "Angelica Kauffmann," unpublished doctoral dissertation, Princeton University, 1969

—, "Charles Rollin and Early Neo-classicism," *Art Bulletin,* XLIX (1967), p. 124

Walpole, Horace, *Anecdotes of Painting in England,* London, 1765

Watt, Alexander, "Paris Commentary," *Studio,* CLVIII (1959), pp. 89–90

Weale, W. H. James, "Simon Binnink, Miniaturist," *Burlington Magazine,* VIII (1905–1906), pp. 355–356

Werner, Alfred, "Paula Modersohn-Becker: A Short, Creative Life," *American Artist,* XXXVII (1973), pp. 16–23, 68–70

Williamson, George C., "Mr. J. Pierpont Morgan's Pictures, The Early Miniatures, I," *The Connoisseur,* XVI (1906), p. 204

Wittkower, Rudolf and Margot, *Born Under Saturn,* New York, 1963

Woermann, Karl, *Catalogue of the Royal Picture Gallery in Dresden,* trans., Dresden, 1902

Wornum, Ralph Nicholson, *Life and Works of Hans Holbein,* London, 1867

Wydenbruck, Nora, *Rilke, Man and Poet,* London, 1949

Wyman, Lillian Buffum, *Elizabeth Buffum Chace,* Boston, 1914

Zigrosser, Carl, *Prints and Drawings of Kaethe Kollwitz,* New York, 1969

INDEX